In Worship of Shiva

In Worship of Shiva

Shanta Rameshwar Rao

Illustrations by
Badri Narayan

Orient Longman

ORIENT LONGMAN LIMITED

Registered Office
5–9–41/1 Bashir Bagh, Hyderabad 500 029
Other Offices
Kamani Marg, Ballard Estate, Bombay 400 038
17, Chittaranjan Avenue, Calcutta 700 072
160 Anna Salai, Madras 600 002
1/24 Asaf Ali Road, New Delhi 110 002
80/1 Mahatma Gandhi Road, Bangalore 560 001
5–9–41/1 Bashir Bagh, Hyderabad 500 029
Jamal Road, Patna 800 001

ISBN 0 86131 684 5

Book Design : Orient Longman

Phototypeset in Perpetua by Phoenix Phototype Setters,
708, Dalamal Tower, Nariman Point, Bombay 400 021
Printed in India at Printwell,
Laxmi Mills Estate, Mahalaxmi, Bombay 400 011
Published by Orient Longman Limited
Kamani Marg, Ballard Estate, Bombay 400 038

Table of Contents

Colour Plates

Introduction to the Text

Indian Mythology has its setting in a measureless earth teeming with human, animal and plant life, that covers underworlds peopled by demons, snake-people and the souls of the dead. There are many heavens, inhabited by gods too numerous to name, whose traditional number, in fact, is 33 crore or 330 million. Their universe covers limitless space and revolves through countless aeons of time.

It is against this vast cosmic backdrop that the myths told in this book have evolved. They are a few of the best known ones from the thousands that fill the scriptures and living traditions of India—living, because, unlike the stories in many world mythologies, they are still part of an active religious culture that exists to this day.

Drawn for the most part from Sanskrit writings that are thousands of years old, the myths told here take their power and presence from recurrent underlying themes: death, religious devotion, and the individual pursuit of spiritual power. They teach that even gods tremble before the spiritual force acquired by a meditating mortal; that devotion to a god can conquer even death; and, ultimately, that death and life are complementary blessings to be met with equal and total acceptance.

These abstract themes are developed in warmly human narratives that can be read and enjoyed as stories or else used as a base for musing on the powerful philosophical propositions they contain.

In loving memory of
Chedna

Astika and Janamejaya

Deep under the earth is Nagaloka, the world of snakes. It is a strange world of magical beauty. In its silky darkness the colours of the underworld gems gleam and sparkle with the fires concealed in their secret hearts. The snakes who live in this world are rich, richer than the kings and merchant men of the earth, and they are wise and very subtle. Many among them are harmless and kind, but some are vicious and evil. But all the snake folk, at the time that this story begins, carried in their hearts a great fear and sorrow, for they lived under the shadow of a dreadful curse.

Only the small human child who lived in Nagaloka, and whom the snake maidens rocked to sleep in a silver cradle, knew neither fear nor sorrow. He was called Astika. His snake companions loved him, and he grew up sheltered and protected among them.

But there came a time when Astika began to question, to demand to know the truth: why was he different from them all? He would not accept the playful answers the snake maidens gave him. 'Why?' he insisted, 'Tell me why.'

Then the snake maidens took him to his mother, Jaratkaru, the queen of snakes and sister of Sesha, Takshaka and Vasuki, the mighty ones of the snake world, for they realized that he was a child no more and must be told the truth.

'Why am I different?' he asked her. Her eyes were shadowed with secret grief as she answered him: 'It was destiny, my son; it was destiny that willed your birth.'

But that did not satisfy him: 'Why did destiny will my birth?' he demanded with a fierce insistence that frightened her, until at last she told him: 'You were born, Astika, in answer to the mighty Sesha's prayers. For many thousands of years he prayed for the gift of a child who would save the snake race from Kadru's curse.'

'And what is this curse, mother?' asked Astika. So she told him the story.

Aeons ago, when creation was new and the young earth sparkled in the light of the first sun, Kadru, the very first snake, and mother of all snakes, sat upon an enormous egg. After five hundred years had gone by, the egg hatched and out of it crawled baby snakes in their thousands. Kadru's heart was glad to see them.

But the gods watching from the heavens could not share her joy. They saw how the snakes would multiply in numbers; they saw how their strength and cunning and their deadly poisons would be a threat to gods and humans alike. They saw that if the snake race were allowed to continue, a day would surely come when they would cause the human race to be wiped out from the face of the earth. And so they determined that the snakes must be destroyed.

But Kadru knew nothing of the fears in the minds of the gods, or of the secret plans they were making. She was young and very lovely, and as she watched the snake children play in and out among the rocks and trees, as she saw them glisten in the water and bask in the warm sunshine, she felt herself blessed a thousand times over. She laughed in her happiness, and grew reckless in her pride. When her sister Vinata came to visit her she boasted without thinking. As the two of them, both wives of Kashyapa, sat together on a rock talking, Kadru's tongue ran away with her. Presently they saw a shining horse come galloping out of the sky.

'Why, it is Uchchaishravas!' said Kadru with a knowing air, 'the heavenly horse that was churned out of the ocean of milk . . . .' Suddenly she turned her dark, flashing eyes upon Vinata and laughed: 'What do you know about these things, you poor creature? I am the clever one. All the world knows it.'

Vinata cast her eyes down modestly and Kadru laughed again. 'I even know the colour of the hairs in Uchchaishravas' tail!'

'Oh no,' breathed Vinata, 'that couldn't be true!'

'The hairs in his tail are black. You didn't know that, did you?'

Vinata was startled; she began to laugh. 'Oh no, Kadru,' said Vinata, 'the hairs in Uchchaishravas' tail should be white. . . .'

'Will you challenge me, foolish girl?' cried Kadru in sudden anger. Her lovely eyes sparked fire. She tossed her proud head. 'Look, I accept your challenge! The one who is proved wrong shall serve as the other's slave for a thousand years. What do you say, Vinata?'

Vinata nodded. 'Why, yes,' she agreed, 'if you say so.' And the horse went flashing by.

That night Kadru crept out and went to look more closely at the

horse, and one glance at its tail told her how wrong she had been. It gleamed white in the moonlight with not a single black hair in it, just as Vinata had said. Kadru bit her lip in anger.

'Vinata right and I wrong? And I be her slave! I'd sooner die!' she exclaimed to herself. Quickly she decided to set matters right. 'I did not hatch all those children for nothing,' she muttered to herself. 'They will help me out of this problem, they must!' And she called them all to her. They came swiftly at her call: Sesha and Vasuki and Takshaka, Kartotaka, Dhananjaya, Kalakeya and all the hundreds and thousands of the snake brothers that she had hatched. 'Listen,' she said, 'do as I command you. Turn yourselves into black hairs with the help of our snake magic, each one of you, and hide among the white hairs in Uchchaishravas' tail.' And she told them about the bet she had taken with Vinata.

The snake children looked at her in astonishment. Then they answered, all speaking together: 'Why, that is a false thing to do. We will not stoop to such a thing!'

'*Will not! Will not!*' repeated Kadru, her eyes opening wide. She could not believe what she had heard. Then a savage anger twisted her features. 'Will not!' she screamed and suddenly she began to dance a demented dance, raving and ranting, weeping and tearing her hair in her hysterical frenzy. 'Will not, did you say? And do you dare to disobey the mother who gave birth to you and nursed and nurtured you? Do you? Do you?'

Her voice rose to a piercing shriek: 'May you die, every single one of you. May you perish in the flames of King Janamejaya's sacrificial fire. May his hatred pursue you to the ends of the earth! May you be annihilated, burnt to ashes.' She paused for breath. There was a pinpoint of time in which she came suddenly face to face with herself, as if hidden hands held up a mirror before her. In that very same instant she saw, far in the blue heavens, a glow and a movement of wings. Her breath caught in her throat, as she realized that the gods had gone by in their golden chariots just as she had uttered her curse. Horror and remorse filled her. She pressed her fingers to her erring mouth, for she had just remembered that words have magical powers; she remembered that, as the gods move through the air above, they whisper; 'Let it be so, let it be so,' and that all words spoken at the exact moment that they pass overhead come true. How could she have forgotten?

Fear possessed her, and helplessly she turned this way and that, like a blind creature caught in a trap. She began to weep and the

4

sound of her weeping filled earth and heaven. Her frightened children crowded round her. 'Fall to the ground,' she cried to them, 'and beg the gods for mercy.' They did so, and she knelt with them and lifted her streaming face to heaven.

The gods heard them, and paused, hovering in the air. Their answering voices chanted: 'The gods are only instruments of destiny, Kadru, and what has happened *had* to happen. It was we who made you speak as you did.'

She stood stunned before them. Then she began to cry piteously. 'This cannot be true. This *cannot* be true. Why did you make me do this terrible thing?' she sobbed. 'Why did you not stop me?'

'The gods are not obliged to answer questions,' murmured the shining ones, 'but we shall answer yours.' They told her how it had happened: 'If the snake race were allowed to multiply, the reptiles would take over heaven and earth,' they murmured. 'The snakes had to be destroyed or they would destroy the world!'

Kadru lifted her eyes to theirs. They were wet with tears and swollen with weeping. Now there was amazement and indignation in them. 'And so you chose *me, their mother,* to curse them!' Anger and sorrow struggled in her voice. '*A mother to curse her children?* You put the words into my mouth? *You* contrived the whole situation? the heavenly horse? the foolish wager? the curse? Oh how could you do it? How could you do something so cruel?'

She sank to the earth and began to sob bitterly. 'There was no other way, Kadru,' murmured the gods shamefacedly. 'The snakes are too strong and too many. Their venom is deadly and sure. When they strike they do so noiselessly and swiftly and they glide away without a sound. Nothing can withstand the power of the snake, except a mother's curse. Deadlier than any weapon, more potent than any incantation of seer or sage, a mother's curse can reduce the universe and all things in it to ash. Though we are gods, Kadru, we had no alternative, and so we caused you to curse your children.'

She hid her face in her hands and she cried out to them to spare her children, begged them not to shut their ears to an anguished mother's prayer.

So long and so piteously did the snake mother beg that even the gods were moved to pity. They lifted the mists from her eyes, and she saw the future before her. She saw in it that there was hope for the snake people, and Brahma, the god of creation, spoke to her: 'There will come one,' Brahma said, 'who will save the snake folk. He will be human though born of a snake woman and he will save his mother's people.' The holocaust could not be prevented, Brahma went on, but the snake race would live.

Kadru was comforted. Destiny would run its course, but a ray of hope shone through the darkness of her despair. Then the mists came up again like a curtain before her eyes and the gods floated away.

The boy Astika listened to his mother's story, and drank in every word. Now he was beginning to understand. He was beginning to see why, despite all the wealth and treasure they possessed, despite all their art and skill and their vast knowledge, the snake folk had this secret sadness in their hearts.

Astika kissed his mother gently and left her. He needed silence and tranquillity in which to think. He began to wander away by himself. When his snake companions called him to join in their sport, Astika shook his head and would not go. When the snake girls came crowding round him begging him to dance and sing and play with them, he excused himself gently and slipped away. Inside him a hundred restless questions demanded answers and solutions.

'A holocaust,' his mother had said. 'The mighty fire sacrifice of Janamejaya . . . .' He whispered the name to himself. Janamejaya, Janamejaya. It had a fierce sound. It rang in his ears like the notes of a gong.

Janamejaya's fire sacrifice!

'Who,' said Astika, 'is this Janamejaya in whom the gods have placed such dreadful power that he can destroy the entire world of snakes? What is his link with our snake people that he should want their destruction?' But no one knew. When he asked his friends they looked at him with frightened eyes. 'It is something terrible in the future,' they answered, 'but what it is, and what it means, we do not know.'

'We must find out then,' said Astika, but they shrank away in fear.

'Hush!' they whispered. 'Do not mention it. Shut your eyes and ears, and do not think about it. If we talk about it there is no knowing what will happen.' But Astika's mind would not let him rest.

'Janamejaya—Janamejaya—who is he?'

And at last he came to Jaratkaru as before, knowing how wise she was, and he asked her. She made him sit beside her and in the silence of the night she continued the story.

There was a king named Parikshit (she began), a human king, young, gallant and quick-tempered, who rode out to hunt one day. Seeing a deer, he followed it into the forest. But though he rode hard and long after it, the deer was too swift for him. Instead, he came upon an ascetic under a tree. Parikshit asked the ascetic if he had seen a deer go past. Once, twice, three times the king repeated the question, but the ascetic failed to answer. How could Parikshit know that this was the sage Shamika? How could he know that in his meditation Shamika had become one with god and totally unconscious of the world around him? The king grew angry and impatient. With his spear he picked up a dead snake that lay on the ground and threw it around the ascetic's neck. Then he galloped away. Shamika still sat in silence, unconscious of insult and outrage.

Just then, young Shringi, the sage's son, came there. He had been away at the time of Parikshit's encounter with Shamika. Shringi had neither his father's wisdom nor patience. 'An insult!' Shringi thundered, 'Parikshit will pay for his arrogance. Within a week from now, Parikshit shall die of the bite of same reptile he has hung on my father's neck. And the snake that will kill him shall be none other than Takshaka, monarch of the serpent world.'

A darkness shadowed the earth as Shringi uttered the words and a cold wind passed over King Parikshit's face. Its touch was like the cold hand of death.

Sitting upon his throne Takshaka heard Shringi's curse and felt its power. Silent and sure, he began to crawl up into the world of men where Parikshit lived.

But when Shamika opened his eyes and saw Shringi's distorted face and heard Shringi's tale, he was very distressed and reproached his son. Shringi tried to defend himself. 'He insulted us,' he said sullenly; 'Because he is rich and we are poor, he mocked us.'

'What have we to do with insult and mockery, Shringi?' Shamika asked him. 'Are we not ascetics and above these things? We must take back the curse.'

'The words have already been spoken,' Shringi muttered. 'Destiny must fulfil itself.'

'I will warn him,' the kindly Shamika persisted. 'Perhaps he will find some way to save himself.' And he sent a messenger to warn the king.

Listening to the messenger's words, Parikshit felt his brave heart shrivel up inside him.

'Death . . . death for me?' he said in a strangled voice. 'But I am

7

young. All my life is ahead of me.' He fell on his knees weeping. 'I am young, and death is for the old, the weary!' But the messenger had slipped away unseen and Parikshit lifted up his face to find himself alone.

Now Parikshit desperately began to look for a way of warding off the death that was in store for him. His ministers and friends, his wives and his family came to him offering advice, telling him of doctors, magicians, sorcerers, faith-healers. He sent messengers scurrying across his kingdom to seek them out and to enlist their services. They came in answer to his summons, flocking to the capital in great numbers. They talked loudly about their skills. They boasted about their ability to cure snake-bite. Seeing them and hearing them, Parikshit felt his fears recede. 'All will be well,' he told himself, but at night as he lay wide-eyed in his bed, the fear returned, and he saw before him Takshaka's scaly form and lidless eyes, the raised hood, and the forked tongue, and he started up in a cold sweat, screaming.

'Dreams . . . only dreams,' he panted in the darkness. 'Soon it will be daylight and there will be nothing to fear.' But daylight and wakefulness brought no relief. He started at every shadow, gasped at every movement and seemed to see the swaying of Takshaka's hood in every fluttering leaf and every falling flower.

'Was there no one who could save the king?' cried Astika.

'All is destiny, my son,' his mother replied sadly. 'No man can defeat destiny.'

Her eyes grew wistful. 'And yet, and yet,' she whispered, 'perhaps he might have been saved.'

And she related to him the story of Kashyapa.

It was rumoured (said she) that Kashyapa knew the secret mantra that could cure snake-bite. From far and near people bitten by snakes used to be brought to Kashyapa to be cured. He healed them, restored them to life, and as they left him, they blessed his name and laid their humble offerings at his feet.

One day, the liveried horsemen sent by King Parikshit came to his door. They handed him the costly presents Parikshit had sent and gave him the royal message. 'Come,' they said, 'there is no time to lose.' Kashyapa glanced at the objects. 'I will come,' he answered at last, and added swiftly, 'but not for the things the king will give me.' He grew a little pompous as he went on: 'To heal and cure is my duty, and the king is a good and noble man.'

8

But after they had gone, Kashyapa's eyes strayed back to the king's gifts. How they glittered; how they seemed to dance before his eyes. He laughed as he thought of the foolish folk who were taken in by outward appearances. Nevertheless it seemed unwise to let them lie around a temptation to thieves and burglars. So Kashyapa collected them together and put them away. Then, taking his staff, he began the long walk to the capital.

As he walked, he saw a little snakeling no bigger than a thumbnail. It was going the same way. Kashyapa smiled to see how small and helpless it was, wriggling in the dust. He would have gone on, but the little snakeling spoke to him. Kashyapa stooped to listen.

'Ah,' said the snakeling, 'what a curious coincidence that you, the healer, and I, the killer, should walk side by side.'

'Killer!' Kashyapa regarded the creature with amusement. He knew that if he chose to, he could crush it to death underfoot. But the snake did not wait for him to choose. Quicker than a blink, it reared up and spread out its hood. The very earth seemed to shake as Kashyapa saw the small, insignificant thing turn into a mighty saffron-coloured monster. And when he saw the crown upon its snake-head, he knew that it was Takshaka, monarch of the snake world, who stood before him. He saw the fearful, swaying hood rise higher and higher until it was on a level with his face. Their breath mingled. Snakes, yes, Kashyapa had seen thousands, but never before the king of them all! He stared at it fascinated, but unafraid.

There was a hiss in his ear: 'Foolish Kashyapa, do you not realize that my power is greater than yours; that I am Takshaka and no ordinary snake! What chance have you against me? Do you not understand that if you fail in your task, as you surely must, you will be the laughing-stock of all men? Turn back, foolish one, and do not attempt the impossible.' 'I will not fail, Takshaka,' Kashyapa answered quietly.

The snake king laughed a soundless laugh: 'Shall I show you my power?' His eyes gleamed maliciously. He streaked away past Kashyapa's bare feet and the next minute the sage saw him coiled at the foot of a giant banyan-tree. His raised hood swayed and in the air all around was the wild sound of snake melodies from invisible pipes.

'My power . . .' Takshaka whispered again, 'shall I show you my power?' And swifter than lightning he struck the tree. A groan of anguish went through its giant frame and it shuddered visibly. The flames leaped from it, and poison-fumes, dark and foul, rose up like fog, sending all living things scurrying away in fear to escape death. Kashyapa saw how the green leaves of the tree shrivelled up and died; how the great branches withered; how the bark peeled off and fell away.

The snake stretched his golden hood towards Kashyapa. His forked tongue flicked in and out; his body quivered with his cruel soundless laughter. 'Tremble before me, Kashyapa, and do not attempt to pit your strength against mine,' he hissed.

'You are very sure of yourself, are you not?' Kashyapa's answering voice was heavy with scorn. 'Well, I will show you, king of crawling serpents; I will show you something you have not seen before.'

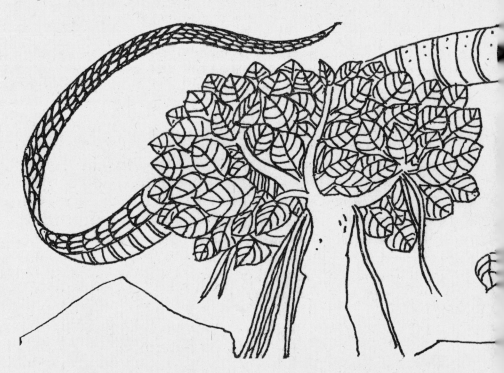

He sat cross-legged on a rock and closed his eyes. His body grew rigid; his eyeballs rolled up behind his closed lids; breath ceased, and presently the words of a mantra set the air rippling with its magic.

A dart of fear shot through Takshaka's cold snake-heart. He stared before him unable to believe his eyes. For his mighty work of death was being undone. The dead tree was reviving to the words of Kashyapa's prayer. The earth where it stood was growing moist and fragrant, and a small shoot was pushing its way up, tender and green. Life was springing out of death.

When Kashyapa opened his eyes he saw the snake all agitated and

10

flustered. 'There must be some mistake,' Takshaka whispered, staring at the tree he had killed. It was growing, its soft green tendrils thrusting upwards. Soon it was a full-sized banyan, with many roots stretched downwards from its branches like the arms of dancers, its green foliage rustling happily in the breeze, and its small, round, red figs glistening in the sunlight.

'Do you see?' said Kashyapa. He faced the snake king calmly, and Takshaka hid his crowned head in shame and lay low in the dust. 'Do you see how the power of healing triumphs over the power of death?'

'It's not true, it can't be true!' Takshaka sobbed. A hundred

conflicting thoughts were swarming in his snake-mind. He felt weak and foolish, and, in the secret depths of his mind he was thinking: '*If I do not do something, this village doctor will cure Parikshit and where shall I be? If Kashyapa's mantra revives those whom I strike dead, nobody will fear me. If I do not do something at once, will he not scatter Shringi's curse to the winds, stop the course of destiny and bring my name to dust?*'

Very softly, with all the cunning at his command, the snake king began to talk, words so smooth, so sweet, that Kashyapa felt their subtle power steal through his iron will. He struggled against it.

'I must not give in,' he whispered to himself. He turned this way and that, but his movements were like those of a fly caught in a jar of honey. And the smooth voice of the snake went on and on talking sweetly, lovingly. It talked of gifts.

'I am rich,' whispered Takshaka, 'richer than Parikshit; richer than all the kings of the world. I will shower you with gifts and make you rich.'

'No!' cried Kashyapa, stopping his ears with his fingers. But, as he stared avidly at the jewelled crown on Takshaka's head, his mind was already beginning to cry out: 'I am a poor man. I have done so much for others, but what have I ever got for my pains? Why should I always live in poverty?'

He shut his eyes, but he could not shut out the sparkle and glint of the gems in Takshaka's crown. He began to argue, to reason with himself. 'Who am I to work against destiny?' he asked. 'How can I attempt to hold back the course of fate?' And while he was reasoning and debating with himself, he did not realize that he had turned and was walking back homewards, away from Parikshit's capital. He walked like a man held in a spell, while the snake voice whispered, sweetly caressing, gently enticing: 'Go home, go back home. I will give you wealth. You will never be poor any more . . . .'

In his palace Parikshit waited for Kashyapa and he waited in vain.

However, he was not idle. Fear would not let him rest. A thousand plans went through his mind like black mice scurrying round and round in a dark room. Destiny must be defeated. His friends and well-wishers brought him their solutions. They built him a house: an extraordinary house, on a single tall pillar with armed guards standing all around it, charged with the task of keeping out strangers. A clever house it was, designed to cheat fate and keep death away.

'You will be safe in here,' gloated the clever folk who built it, and hope fluttered feebly in poor Parikshit's heart.

He shut himself up in the house and would not come out. But fear followed him like a shadow and would not leave him even here.

'Make offerings in the temples. Distribute gold and silver as alms to the poor, order prayers to be repeated ceaselessly day and night.' The wise and clever gave advice and suggestions. They were never at a loss. But deep in Parikshit's heart his fear crouched, waiting. And he sat sweating on the edge of his throne, turning the prayer beads in his clammy fingers and crying out for time. Each day, as it wound its tortured way to sundown, seemed like a year. But there was no sign of any snake.

12

'Calm yourself,' said his friends. 'Those were a madman's words. Will you lose your sleep over them?'

Parikshit managed a smile. It was a weak, sickly smile and it died in the very moment of its birth. Enviously he stared at the carefree faces of the people around him. They seemed to him like dream faces from an unreal world. For him there was only the reality of fear: 'Snakes,' he quavered piteously, 'keep them away. Do not let one enter. Do not let it kill me.'

'But no snake has been seen anywhere in the neighbourhood, O mighty vanquisher of foes,' his courtiers protested, amused. 'Not so much as a small grass snakeling.'

Nevertheless he began to count the hours in his mind, and suddenly with mounting joy realized that the agony was nearly at an end. Six whole days had gone by. Six tortured sleepless nights were over: there was one last night and one last day that remained, and when he had tided over those he would have peace for evermore.

He began to feel lighter. The night passed and the last morning dawned, a clear, beautiful day, bright as a jewel. The sun climbed high. There was no sign of Takshaka. A golden afternoon settled upon them, and the courtiers lolled about in their chairs in drowsy, heavy contentment. Still no Takshaka. As evening drew on, the servants moved about in the extraordinary house, lighting the lamps. Music played and then came the chant of evening prayers. From the women's apartments there came the sounds of laughter and tinkling anklets. All was at peace. Parikshit felt the gentleness of the evening steal into his weary heart. How foolish he had been!

His courtiers sat around him: he could not bear to be alone. An hour more, perhaps a half hour, and the danger would have passed; even its memory would fade away! A tiny, tiny voice whispered deep inside him: 'But there is still that hour to go. You must not relax. You must watch, watch, watch ceaselessly.'

'There is no telling when the snake might come,' murmured Parikshit. His courtiers laughed: 'If Takshaka had to come he would have done so by now. Your fears are groundless. The sun will soon go down now. Take heart, sir. There is nothing to fear.'

Presently their laughter grew louder. 'Now that the danger is over,' they went on uproariously, 'we must celebrate!' And they slapped each other on the back. 'Takshaka has been thwarted and we have won.' Their gaiety was infectious. Parikshit began to laugh with them, fearfully at first and then with growing courage.

'Yes, we have won.' He threw back his bared chest and said

aloud: 'Takshaka has been defeated!' He ordered the servants to bring in food and drink: 'Let us celebrate! The days of waiting are over!' And as if heaven had heard his wish, at that very moment someone announced the arrival of a party of strangers with baskets of fruit for the king. They were standing waiting below at the foot of the column where the guards had detained them. 'Strangers!' growled one of the courtiers, suddenly suspicious. 'But no strangers are allowed near this house.' Instantly Parikshit tensed and his eyes darted this way and that. He began to tremble. 'Who are these strangers?'

'Simple forest tribesmen,' was the reply, 'loyal subjects of the king. They have brought him fruit!'

'Ho,' said the wise and clever men, warily. 'These are stories we have heard before. Do they think they can fool us?' And they ordered that every one of the baskets be uncovered and examined. 'Who knows? There may be a snake hidden somewhere. We will take no chances.' The guards were set to search the baskets. They searched with great care in the straw. They searched and peered at each fruit, turning it round in their hands, smelling it, holding it to their ears. But they found no snake in the baskets, only luscious, golden-ripe fruit, fit for kings to eat. No one noticed the lidless eyes of the tribesmen, their scaly skins, their soft hissing voices. The servants trooped in, bearing great silver dishes piled high with the fruit. When they laid the dish before Parikshit he chose a few of the fruits with his own royal hands and offered them to the assembled nobles.

'No, no, you must eat first,' they protested. He looked at the fruit and was tempted.

He laughed and they chorused: 'The most beautiful of them all for you, sir.' He took the most beautiful fruit of all and leaned back on his throne. With a silver knife he peeled the skin and let it spiral softly down into the silver dish. He regarded the flesh inside with a warm glow of satisfaction: it was as sound as the skin was beautiful. Opening his mouth wide, he bit into it, the rich sweet juice filling his thirsty mouth. He bit again and again. Greedily he ate; the sweet flesh melted in his mouth and the juice spurted out and trickled down. He sucked at its sweetness, sucked and sucked as if he had been starving, until suddenly the core of the fruit was bared. He smiled as he saw the seed embedded in it. Dreams flitted through his mind: that little seed contained the germ of life; it held the future. If he planted it there would be a sapling that would grow into a tree.

14

There would be fruit on the tree and seeds in the fruit. From the seeds would come more trees. There would be an orchard. Suddenly the smile froze on his lips. A thought rose trembling to his mind. A voice inside him shrieked: 'What was that movement at the core, just under the seed—was it, was it a live creature? Was it, was it—a snake?' His mouth gaped open, but no sound came from his throat. He stared, white and cold, at that one point in the fruit, and all else lost meaning and significance. He began to shake in every limb.

And then a courtier's voice came, as if from a distance: 'A maggot? A maggot in the king's fruit? How could this have been allowed to happen?'

Parikshit saw what a fool he had been to take a maggot for a snake. Cold drops of sweat stood out on his brow, but his relief was so great that he could have danced, flung out his arms and leaped up in the air. He began to shake with laughter. He held the half-eaten fruit in his hand and laughed. He could not stop laughing. 'What a joke! What a wonderful joke!' and the tears ran down his face. 'For seven days we have waited for the mighty Takshaka—and now see who is here!' He was laughing so much that his hands were unsteady as he scooped the maggot out on the point of the silver knife and held it out for the people to see. They roared with him. Their voices resounded through the house. The ladies in their curtained apartments heard them and, hiding their painted faces behind their pretty jewelled hands, laughed merrily at the joke. The servants, unable to contain their mirth, fell on each other, laughing. The guards at the foot of the column heard the story and, holding their sides, shook with great, booming laughter. 'A maggot!' gasped Parikshit, helpless with laughing. 'Oh, I've never laughed so much in my life!'

A courtier reeled forward and pointed drunkenly at the creature. 'Perhaps he thinks he's Takshaka!' he guffawed and fresh gales of laughter greeted his words, with Parikshit laughing the loudest.

'Perhaps!' Parikshit agreed, wiping the tears from his eyes. With an effort he controlled himself. Holding the knife up and looking at the little golden creature curled on it, he addressed it with a great show of solemnity, for now he had thought of a new game to keep up the joke.

'Perhaps, little one, *you* are Takshaka?' He chuckled and went on: 'Perhaps you have come to kill me?' Still chuckling, he took the maggot between his finger and thumb. Dramatically he raised it to his neck. 'Well so be it, little creature. You shall be Takshaka for a while! You shall be king for a day!' The assembly clapped their hands, delighted that they were about to witness a new piece of acting. In the same solemn voice, Parikshit intoned: 'If you are Takshaka, little one, then here is my throat and strike me dead!'

Laughter again, uproarious laughter. Only Parikshit had stopped laughing. His horrified eyes were staring before him. The maggot . . . .

'No,' he cried, but his voice stuck in his throat, 'No, no, it's not true.'

But it was. The maggot was swelling. It was as long and thick as his finger now; the next minute it was as big as his arm. It was true . . . . The maggot had become a snake—a saffron-coloured monster with flicking tongue and cold, cruel eyes.

'Takshaka?' Through chattering teeth and constricted throat, Parikshit's voice cried out, 'It's Takshaka! Oh help me. Save me! Help!'

But no one heard him. They were still laughing. Were they blind, and deaf—to leave him so, looking alone into the eyes of death!

He heard its savage hiss; felt its poisoned breath. Then mustering up all his failing strength he cried out, and this time they turned.

'Takshaka!' The courtiers screamed. Then confusion and panic; everyone running helter-skelter. Parikshit was forgotten, left alone again with the great red-gold hood swaying before his eyes.

'Not now, not now!' he sobbed, pleading with the horrible thing. 'Give me time—a few years—a few months—a few weeks; days— *one* day, give me *one* day—oh give me an *hour*, *one* hour . . . .'

The snake struck, and an awful, agonized cry shook the rafters. The stunned courtiers saw the king writhing as the poison raced through his veins . . . .

Then mercifully it was over, and the courtiers drew near, approaching the prostrate body fearfully. They stood in frightened groups staring, pointing, whispering: 'The king! The king is dead!' His crown had rolled away and he lay quite stiff and still. After a while they began to ask: 'Where is the killer? We must find the killer.' They began to bustle about. They brought sticks and stones to kill him. But the killer was gone. No one had seen him go. So they approached the body of Parikshit, weeping and wailing loudly, protesting their love for him.

'It was a cruel fate for a king to die in this way, and his only fault a quick temper,' said Astika. His voice was low, his eyes full of compassion.

16

'Listen,' Jaratkaru answered gently, 'Hear what happened then. The story has not ended.'

King Parikshit had a son, Janamejaya—a child at the time of his father's death. He grew up in the lonely, sad palace, wondering why he must sit on a throne too big for him, instead of playing with his companions as he longed to do. And when the child heard the story of how the snake Takshaka had wormed his stealthy way into his father's stronghold and struck him unawares, he swore, with the hot tears streaming down his face, that he would not rest until he had avenged his father's death, until he had destroyed, annihilated, burnt to ashes the entire race of snakes.

'I shall conduct a mighty sacrifice,' said Janamejaya, 'Agni shall aid me. The snakes of the earth will die in its raging fires. And of them all, of the thousands and thousands of them all, one especially shall be my target—Takshaka! Wherever Takshaka hides I shall find him and bring him to his death. For Takshaka, my father's killer, there shall be no refuge. My anger will hound him to the remotest corners of the universe, and I shall destroy him though I die in the attempt.' Little did Janamejaya realize that he was no more than a tool in destiny's hands, helping to bring about the fulfilment of Kadru's old, old curse.

Jaratkaru's story came to its end. She looked anxiously at her son. But for a long while he made no movement. His eyes looked out, dark and distant with thought. It was hours before the boy turned slowly to face her. 'And now for my own story, mother,' he said, 'Tell me, why was I born? Why did destiny will my birth? Why am I different from you and from all our people? Why do strange dreams invade my nightly sleep and strange thoughts disturb my waking hours?'

He looked down unhappily at his limbs, clumsy outgrowths jointed to a trunk that utterly lacked the flowing grace of snakes. She saw that she must tell him. She could put it off no longer. And so she began the story.

Astika was born in answer to mighty Sesha's prayer. When the gods left Kadru, her children dispersed, all except the three eldest, who were bent on finding some way to save the snake folk from extinction. Sesha, the eldest, determined that he would pray for them. He left his kingdom and became an ascetic. Many followed in his path and went with him into the forests. Takshaka, the second, ascended the throne and became king. The third snake brother, Vasuki, declared that he too would stay among his people.

In his mind Vasuki thought over and over again of the words of the gods.

A child, they had said, a boy, born of a snake girl and a human father would save the snake race. 'A snake girl . . . a snake girl.' Vasuki remembered his little sister. He loved her deeply. 'Jaratkaru' he had wanted her to be named when she was still a baby, and so she had been named that.

Jaratkaru. It was a strange, harsh name and Vasuki could not say why he had thought of it. A voice had seemed to whisper insistently in his heart at the time that she was born: 'Jaratkaru. Name her Jaratkaru.' She grew in beauty and grace, and as her gentle brother watched the swift rippling movements of her brown and gold body, he knew she was the answer to his prayer. 'She shall live in my home,' said Vasuki. 'I shall look after her and bring her up.' So Jaratkaru, mother of Astika, grew up under wise Vasuki's care.

One soft spring day, she woke up after a long sleep and felt in her snake blood the call of springtime. Her body began to uncoil itself and noiselessly she glided away out of Vasuki's palace home, and moved up a hole to emerge into the world of humans. On and on she glided, until she found herself in a forest grove, and there she stopped suddenly when she saw a man. He was sitting under a tree, his legs crossed and his eyes closed. His ribs showed starkly under his sun-blackened skin and, as she gazed at him, she knew that this was the man she must marry.

Then softly she uttered magic words, until her snake form gave place to a human form, and she stood before him in all her alluring beauty. The man opened his eyes and scowled when he saw her.

'Out, out, woman,' he rasped angrily. 'Get out of my sight.' But she stood there before him with downcast eyes and she would not move. And as he began to grow conscious of her loveliness, he became angrier than ever because it disturbed him.

She joined her hands and spoke to him. She told him of her love and begged him to marry her.

'Marry you!' repeated the sage and his anger gave place to amusement. He grimaced at her, showing his toothless gums. 'Ho! Ho!' he chuckled. 'Did you say love, woman? And did you talk of marriage? Do you not see, foolish one, that I am an ascetic and care nothing for home or family or the comforts of domestic life? What

happiness do you expect from marriage with an ascetic?'

But she only looked on him with eyes of love and worship, and would not go from him though he waved her away with an impatient hand.

Suddenly he shot a sharp, mocking glance at her.

'What is your name, woman?' he demanded. She opened her lips to speak, but before she could do so a deep voice answered: 'Mighty sage, her name is the same as yours: Jaratkaru.'

Jaratkaru trembled, and the sage started. It was Vasuki who had spoken. She had not seen him come, but he had followed her and now lay coiled at the sage's feet and was speaking in a human voice.

The sage began to shake with laughter again as at a great joke. 'Why,' said he, 'I have travelled far and wide for many years and never have I found, till today, a woman with the same name as mine.' He paused and fixed her with his bird-like gaze: 'I will marry her,' he announced, so unexpectedly that she trembled again, this time in bewilderment. But he went on speaking to Vasuki as if she was not there at all: 'This is what I swore to myself and to the spirits of my ancestors long ago when I was young. I had no wish to marry but they cried out to me from the twilight world of the dead, where they lived in torment, begging me to take a wife and give them children and grandchildren to carry on their name. So, to satisfy them, I took an oath that I would obey them. But only on one condition: the woman I would marry must have the same name as I. That satisfied them, and they ceased to torment and pester me. I went my way. I looked for such a woman but never did I find her till today.' The ascetic's eyes travelled again over the snake girl's form. 'And now she has come, and I see that I must marry her.' He laughed his harsh laugh again, and rolled the name on his tongue. 'The same name . . . is that not as good a reason as any to marry a woman?' he asked sharply.

'As good as any,' Vasuki answered humbly. 'My sister shall be your wife, great one: it is for this that she had been born and bred.'

The sage gave him a quick look. 'Yes,' he said, 'it is part of the prophecy. So for a year we will be married, and that will serve our purpose, Vasuki—yours and mine. There will be a son.' The old man's eyes returned to the snake maiden, and he regarded her loveliness and youth. 'Do you hear, Jaratkaru? A son will be born to us, during that year.' Suddenly he grew serious. His face took on a fierce intensity: 'I have spent long years in prayer and meditation,' he told them gravely. 'I have acquired great merit through my asceticism. I have no worldly wealth to give to my son, but he shall inherit the fruits of my ascetic life. All the merit of my long years of prayer shall be his for he will need to be strong. He will be the answer to the mighty prayers of Sesha, the great brother of all the snakes, he who supports the reclining Vishnu himself. And he will save your people from Kadru's curse.'

And so they were married, Jaratkaru the ascetic and Jaratkaru the snake. The bent, gaunt old man came with his lovely bride and Vasuki to the snake kingdom, and lived there among the snakes. Jaratkaru loved him and served him dutifully. But a day came when he grew tired of her love; when the palace seemed like a prison to him and he longed again for the wandering life of an ascetic. Then he found some excuse to be annoyed with her, and he left her and her palace and fled, never more to return. She wept sad tears, but when she saw that she carried his child in her womb, her heart took comfort.

As the story came to an end Jaratkaru smiled into her son's face, but his eyes were full of thought. Again, it was a long time before he spoke.

'I see my path now, mother,' he said, 'I see what I must do: I must leave this country of my mother's people and make my way into the world of human beings. I must follow in my father's footsteps and live the ascetic's life. This is the destiny I see before me; and into that destiny I must weave the destinies of the snakes, my kinsmen. I see now that I must save the snake race.'

She knew this was true. She had always known the day would come when he would leave her. She held him close and kissed his dear face. For the last time she fed him with food lovingly prepared with her own caring hands. And then she let him go. As long as she could see it, she followed his blurred figure receding in the distance.

In the world of humans Astika travelled far and wide looking for the father whom he had never seen. He never found him, and at last he gave up the search. But during his wanderings he lived among people and learned many things. He saw how between them and his mother's people there was suspicion, mistrust and fear. He saw men killing snakes, torturing and tormenting them, allowing them no peace or rest, and his heart cried out against these things. And all the while he knew in his heart that he must save them from the curse of Kadru.

One day he went into a forest grove and took his seat beneath a

banyan tree. He had determined to prepare for a great penance. The penance he felt, was necessary if he was to save the snakes, his brothers. He smiled sadly as he thought of their jewelled beauty. Poisonous, yes, and evil, but only some of them; and these poisonous ones were so beautiful that to kill them would be mortal sin. If for no other reason, for their beauty alone they deserved to live. But many of them were dull and drab. They lived out their timid, uneventful days on earth hurting no one. They too were his brothers. He had loved and played with them. They had no poison. They lived on rats, frogs, mice and other such creatures that plagued the human folk. If all snakes vanished, then would these things not swell in numbers unchecked? Would they not then become a pestilence? And if all snakes were destroyed what would eagles feed on? Would they not need to turn to unnatural food? Baby goats, perhaps, or new-born lambs? And would this not be evil? Where would all this end? Astika thought deeply about these things and he became more and more convinced that the hand of god was everywhere in nature, keeping a balance.

He began to see all creatures, and not only snakes, as his kinsmen, his brothers: like himself they too had been given the right to live and flourish. He saw how all things in nature were interdependent. What a beautiful and wondrous thing was creation, from the humblest ant among the blades of grass to the mighty whale in the ocean's depths! He closed his eyes and began to pray.

In the palace, Janamejaya, the king, was praying too, and this was his impassioned prayer:

'My oath, heavenly beings: may I never be false to my word.' Through the days and nights of many years, he had never forgotten that oath, but had held fast to it, nursing his great anger in his heart. And all the while he prepared for the mighty sacrifice of snakes. The day came at last when Janamejaya sent out his heralds to tell the people, to have them rally around: the sacrifice was about to begin. The message went out with drums and bugles, trumpets and horns, calling all people who knew magic and sorcery and snake-craft to come to the palace; all priests and wizards and snake-charmers were wanted. They came to the palace bringing with them their potions and magic mixtures, their charms and talismans, reciting magic words.

'Nothing must go wrong,' Janamejaya commanded. 'All things must be carefully, meticulously planned. There must be no mistake.'

'There shall be no mistake,' they promised.

Then on an auspicious day the priests announced that the hour had come: the sacrifice must begin.

King Janamejaya, dressed in spotless white, took his place beside the consecrated hearth. His face was set, his eyes grim. His hands did not falter as he struck the flints together to start the sacrificial fire. The sparks flew. The twigs caught fire. The flames leaped up. And the strange echoes of Kadru's ancient curse pierced the air: 'May you be destroyed, annihilated, burnt to ashes.'

Presently a snake, a little green and yellow snake, came flying on the wind. It threw itself into the fire where it curled to a black cinder. Another followed, and another. The king sat very still and straight and his vow repeated itself in his heart like the refrain of a madman's song. A wind rose up from the north; then other winds from east and west and south began to blow, and on these winds came more snakes who fell into the great fire. First they came singly, then in pairs; and then in fours, fives, scores, and finally in hundreds—snakes of many colours, of many sizes, five-hooded, seven-hooded, dragon-faced serpents, hamadryads, boa constrictors, pythons, and kraits, glowing jewel-like, twisting, curling, writhing; rattlesnakes, rock-snakes, tree-snakes, water-snakes, old and young snakes and baby snakes scarcely out of their eggs. It seemed as if there was no end to the reptiles as they came hurling themselves to their death and destruction. Janamejaya's face showed no emotion. Not a muscle moved. The cries of the bereaved ones in the snake world reached his ears, but in his heart there was only one thought repeating itself: 'Though heaven and earth be destroyed in the holocaust, the sacrifice shall not be ended; though every living thing should be wiped off the earth's face, this sacrifice shall go on. It shall continue until every living snake—until Takshaka himself—has been annihilated.'

Pale and trembling, Takshaka, monarch of snakes, clung to his throne. He felt the power of Janamejaya's magic pulling him and he struggled against it and against his growing helplessness. All around him in the caverns of the snake world the magic spells were calling and the snakes were being lifted up and carried away on the wings of the wind. The wind was a gale now, lashing the trees. How long would he withstand it? 'What shall I do? Where shall I hide from my doom?' wept Takshaka.

And then he remembered his friend, Indra, rich, powerful and secure in his kingdom in heaven. In a flash Takshaka uncoiled

himself, and took a flying leap into the air. The next minute he was in Indra's courtroom, at Indra's feet. The snake king crept under his shining throne. He coiled himself around one of its legs and lay there trembling. 'Whatever happens,' he thought wretchedly, 'I must not let go.'

'Where is Takshaka?' thundered Janamejaya, pouring butter into the sacrifical fire. By now it was as big as a mountain with its flames seeming to touch the sky. And when he heard that Takshaka had fled from the snake country and taken refuge in Indra's heaven, he laughed scornfully. 'Increase the magic incantations a thousandfold and then more,' he commanded. 'For Takshaka there shall be no mercy. He who brought about my father's death shall not be allowed to escape. And if Indra has offered him refuge then Indra shall be destroyed with him!'

The priests brought out more powerful spells than any heard of before. Their voices rang out over earth, sea and sky.

'No, no, no!' cried Takshaka as their power reached him under Indra's throne. 'Indra, protect me!'

Indra felt a movement beneath his throne, felt the throne rise up in the air and glide down towards the earth!

He looked about him in panic, understanding nothing.

Then he saw the snake king and he realized what was happening.

'Oh Takshaka! Takshaka!' he whimpered, 'See what you have done! Now, not only you, but I must die too! Do you not see, Takshaka, that if I try to save you then I shall be destroyed with the snakes in Janamejaya's fire?'

'I have taken refuge with you, Indra,' Takshaka pleaded. 'Do not, I beg you, do not forsake me!'

And all the while they were speaking, Indra's throne went gliding earthwards!

'I must forsake you, Takshaka,' Indra cried out miserably. 'I have no wish to die. You must let me go!' And even as he said it, Takshaka's hold on the throne began to slip, and, with Indra seated upon it the throne began to soar upwards, while Takshaka was left helpless and alone in the air, going surely down! Now Takshaka knew his end was very near and he cried out to the gods for mercy.

Astika opened his eyes as he emerged from his meditation. His mind was wonderfully clear now, clear as the mountain air. The earth around him sparkled in the morning sunshine. Astika's heart sang at its loveliness. But even as Astika rejoiced, there came to his ears the sound of weeping and wailing. Then there was a great

rushing wind that screamed around him, like a demon. It was full of magic spells of hatred, and he saw the fearful sight of snakes being carried upon that wind and Astika realized that they were being carried to their destruction in Janamejaya's fire sacrifice. Suddenly he knew what he must do. He took up his beggar's bowl and staff, and began to walk swiftly towards Janamejaya's palace. At its gates the guards stopped him.

'Who are you, stranger?' they demanded. 'Do you not know that the king has ordered that no one should be allowed into the gates of the palace? Do you not know that the snake sacrifice is being conducted and the king wants no interruption?'

'I am an ascetic,' Astika answered. 'I have spent long years in meditation. I must see the king. My business cannot wait.' They looked at his face and grew uneasy at what they saw there—the clear, piercing gaze of his eyes, the strength of his mouth, the snake marks upon his brow. They moved aside and let him pass. 'An ascetic's wishes must not be crossed. Some harm will surely come to all of us if we stop him,' they whispered to each other. 'This is no ordinary man!'

Astika went striding through the halls, past long lines of priests who stood chanting. He entered the courtyard where the sacrificial fire blazed. He stood among the people and looked about him. Even from the distance at which he stood he could see Janamejaya's fierce, hate-filled face. Though the king's eyes were closed he could see the glow of the fire reflected in their depths.

Astika turned his gaze upon the people. How they pressed close to each other, drunk with excitement, crying, 'Kill, kill, kill! Destroy the snakes! The snakes are our enemies.' Their voices quivered with anger and hatred. 'Look!' they were pointing to the sky. He looked up with them and saw a shining object in the blue like a star. And then as it came swiftly nearer, it looked like a golden bowl. It bobbed up and down, and he saw it was neither star nor bowl, but Indra's throne. And clinging to its leg, weeping piteously, begging Indra to help him, was the mighty monarch of snakes— Takshaka. Astika saw how, in mortal fear of his own skin, Indra refused that help and how his shining throne sailed back to heaven, leaving Takshaka in the air, falling down, down, towards Janamejaya's sacrificial fire.

The people were dancing madly about him, but Astika paid no attention to them. Steadily he pressed forward, until he reached the place of the sacrifice and he stood before the king. The king was

sitting very still and his eyes did not look up. Astika waited for the pause between one chant and the next, and when that instant came, he spoke out, his voice loud and ringing.

'I come for alms, King Janamejaya!'

The king's eyelids flickered. 'You must be a stranger in the city not to know that there will be no favours granted during the days of the sacrifice,' he answered.

'Nevertheless, I must ask,' said Astika, and the king's voice rasped out sharply:

'Who are you? Why are you here?' Loud and clear came Astika's reply: 'I am the sage, Astika, son of Jaratkaru. And I have come to beg for your mercy that the snake people may be spared from further destruction, and that Takshaka, their king, may be allowed to live.'

'Save the snakes!' Janamejaya's voice was scornful. 'Those cruel venomous creatures? Was it not their king that killed my noble father? No, no, ascetic, ask anything but that, for I have vowed to destroy the snake race and leave not one snake alive, not one!' The veins stood out throbbing on his forehead. 'As for Takshaka,' he continued, clenching his fists, 'I shall not rest until I have destroyed him, for he is my enemy above all others.'

Then he made a sign to the priests and they took up their chanting again. Janamejaya poured out the libation. The flames rose, angry and red. Suddenly a shout went up among the people: 'Look, look! There is Takshaka.'

Astika spoke on as if he and Janamejaya were the only two there: 'Janamejaya, I crave mercy for the snakes, for they too are god's creatures.'

'God's creatures?' Janamejaya repeated in a harsh voice. 'Do you call these evil, death-dealing reptiles *god's creatures*? Ah, you must be mad, else how can you not see that snakes are our foremost enemies. Do they not glide noiselessly through the grass and strike innocent men without warning?'

'Nevertheless,' Astika argued, 'nevertheless they too must live. Remember, Janamejaya, that there are many among snakes, many which are harmless and peaceable. Will you destroy all snake life for the sake of some that are poisonous? Is this the creed of a Kshatriya, born to rule justly?'

Janamejaya gave the stranger a quick, sharp glance out of the corner of his eye.

'Ascetic, what are the snakes to you? Why do you come interrupting the sacrifice?' he said.

'They are my kinsmen,' Astika smiled, 'just as they are yours, Janamejaya. Our lives are intertwined, for human beings and snakes depend in mysterious ways upon one another.'

'What madman's talk is this?' said the king, and swung around to face the stranger.

'The fire, the fire,' cried the priests in panic. 'The fire is dying, and must be fed.'

But the king's mind had wandered. The sage's eyes held him. The sage's words had a strange power. He listened and could not turn away. The sage was speaking of love, love for all things. He had a new message for people. He was speaking of the brotherhood of nature's creatures, of man's relationship with life around him—the birds and beasts and plants, trees and grass—yes, even the insects of the air and the fish in the water. Never before had Janamejaya heard such words, ringing with such power and strength. As he listened, Janamejaya forgot the sacrificial fire. Nor did he notice that Takshaka had fallen on the burnt earth and had sped away, making good his escape through a hole at Astika's feet. As Janamejaya listened he felt the power of Astika's wisdom move him, and like the flames of the sacrifice, his anger too began to die down and vanish. Peace stole into his heart. The long day with its agony and pain and tears came to an end. And the night brought rest and peace to the king's cleansed spirit.

Very early the next morning Astika awoke and took his leave of Janamejaya. The king offered him his golden palace and all his wealth, but Astika would not stay. Nor would he let the king renounce these things and accompany him.

'I am an ascetic,' he said, 'born of ascetics, my path is the path of ascetics. But you are a king, and heaven has given you your duty to perform. You must rule the land and guide your subjects and care for their welfare. This is your path, and you must find your salvation in it.'

28

Then he took up his begging bowl and staff and went out of the palace gates. The snake race had been saved. The king and his people accompanied him to the city's limits and watched him go. They saw him take the long hard road, the ascetic's lonely way, and then they turned and went back to the city and the palace.

2

Savitri and Satyavan

The princess Savitri was a ray of sunshine in the lives of her parents. For many years Ashwapati and his queen had been childless, and when Savitri was born, they knew she was an answer to their constant prayers to Savitar, god of the sun. She grew into a lovely girl, marvellously light-limbed and graceful and full of charm. But it was her intelligence and the sun-like brightness of her mind that delighted her father above everything. 'She must have nothing but the best,' he said, and engaged the most learned tutors in the land to teach her and answer her questions.

From her mother she learned to spin and weave and sew, to cook and make a home beautiful and its inmates happy. Her parents loved her and were sad to think that she must be married soon and go from them. They worried, because amongst the princes who ruled the different kingdoms there was not one who seemed worthy of so radiantly lovely a girl as their Savitri. Besides, she herself seemed not to care greatly to have any one of them for her husband, in spite of their wealth and splendour and their armies.

'Send the princess on a grand tour of the land,' said Narada to Ashwapati one day. 'It would be part of her education to see the country, and perhaps, in the course of her travels, she will come across some young man she might like.' And though the suggestion came from Narada, who was a busybody, a trouble-maker, and an incurable gossip, Ashwapati had, in fairness, to admit that it was a good idea. So the arrangements were made, and the princess, accompanied by her retinue, went journeying over the countryside. From far and near the people came to watch as her carriage went by. Sometimes she stopped to talk to them, to join them in their work, to play with their children. Sometimes she sat among them to be entertained by village acrobats and puppeteers, singers and story-tellers. Often they halted at hermitages and pilgrim centres where holy men lived and Savitri spoke to them on serious subjects and listened intently to their discourses. And so she did things she would never have done if she had lived a sheltered life in her father's palace.

One day as they went through a forest they saw a young man walking down the path. He was humbly dressed in the cotton homespun of a working man. Savitri saw him through the curtains of her palanquin and suddenly she knew, as if the gods had whispered it to her, that this was the man she must marry. She ordered her people to halt and sent her messengers to find out who he was.

He was Satyavan, they told her, son of Dyumatsena who had once ruled over an extensive kingdom. But misfortune had come to Dyumatsena: first he had gone blind; then a neighbouring ruler had invaded his land. Satyavan, Dyumatsena and his wife had escaped into the forest to live there in exile and poverty, and there the boy, Satyavan, had grown up working as a forester to provide for his unfortunate parents. Savitri listened to every word, treasuring it in her mind and heart.

'Now my journey has ended,' she thought to herself, and turned to journey back to her father's home. There, she told her parents about Satyavan. They listened, and then they worried for her. A forester son of an impoverished and exiled ruler of an unknown kingdom was hardly what they had in mind for their cherished daughter. He had neither property nor renown, had to support an old mother and a blind father, and lived in a forest hut like an ascetic. What choice was this? And Ashwapati began to doubt his wisdom in having sent his young and impulsive daughter on this wild adventure.

'Are you sure, my child?' he asked her a hundred times. She was. Her answer, though gently spoken, was simple and forthright: 'I have chosen him to be my husband and the father of my children. I have given him my heart.' As they looked at her, her parents sensed the strength and sincerity of her young love, and realized that it was no passing infatuation, no childish fancy.

But when Ashwapati had Satyavan's horoscope read, the astrologers looked distressed.

'Sir, it is better that this marriage does not take place,' they murmured, 'because this man has no more than one year to live.'

Ashwapati was stunned, and Savitri turned pale. When at last Ashwapati spoke, he would not face his daughter: 'You must choose again, Savitri, you have heard what they say.' But Savitri answered: 'Father, I have chosen Satyavan and will not choose another.' She did not falter as she spoke, though her voice was very low. The king

knew that the gentle girl would never be persuaded and he must yield.

The marriage was arranged. That was not difficult. Old Dyumatsena was overjoyed, and gladly agreed to the marriage. An alliance with a ruling monarch as rich, powerful and respected as Ashwapati was beyond all his dreams. As for Satyavan, he confessed that he had loved Savitri from the moment he had seen her. For him there were no doubts. So Savitri and Satyavan were married, with much feasting and singing. Savitri went with her husband and his parents to her new home—a hut in the forest.

'It is a very different life you will lead with us, Savitri, from the one you have known in your father's palace,' Satyavan said to her, as they crossed its threshold. 'Here there will be no servants and maids to attend on you. My parents are old and feeble, and you must look after them and attend to their needs. And a forester's life is not easy. I come home late, and you will have no company but that of the two old people. It's a lonely life you will lead, dear heart.'

For answer she smiled at him and her smile was like sunshine. And soon she made herself at home. As she moved about the house that was now hers, Satyavan was amazed to see the grace, lightness and the delicate skill with which she went about her work. The food that she cooked was wholesome, exquisitely flavoured with the herbs that she gathered outside their cottage. The vessels shone and sparkled, for she scoured and washed them by the brook before filling them with clear, fresh water for the day's use. There were festive rice-paste designs on the threshold and flower and leaf chains on the lintels. She sang as she worked, and the home that had once been silent and isolated became vibrant with the happiness Savitri brought. The old folk loved her and blessed her and Satyavan was happy and proud.

But neither they nor he guessed the secret burden of the knowledge that Savitri carried; no one guessed the reason for the prayers she whispered continuously as she worked. No one knew why each day she woke before dawn to pray, or why each night she spent long hours deep in prayer. No one knew that from the moment the astrologers had revealed to her the future that awaited her husband, she had prayed, with all the intensity of her young and steadfast heart, never to be separated from him. A great faith flowed within her that her love must surely triumph over everything—even death. Satyavan was puzzled, and the old people worried that her health might suffer. But her smile was radiant as she assured them that all would be well: she had made a vow or two which she must fulfil, she said. It was of no importance; they were not to worry. It would not be for long.

So the weeks and months passed and one day Savitri begged of her parents-in-law their blessings upon the very last penance she was about to undertake.

'For three days and nights I must meditate without ceasing,' she said to them, 'and during that time I must fast. I may speak to no one for all my thoughts must be directed heavenwards. Neither may I sleep, for every second is precious and must not be lost.'

They stared at her uncomprehending. 'Child, you are young,' pleaded the old people, 'and these penances are not meant for children. Enjoy the days of your youth, Savitri, for they will not return. 'But I *am* happy,' she protested earnestly, as she bent down in obeisance and touched their feet. The old people raised her and embraced her: 'May the gods grant you your desires,' they said.

33

During the three days and nights that followed, Savitri undertook her great and rigorous penance. First came the bath in the icy waters of the river before the hour of dawn, and then the prayers in the silence and solitude of the forest. As she had vowed she took neither food nor water. Unceasingly she prayed, speaking no word, and allowing nothing to come between her and her god. And when night came, she sat in silent meditation on a rock, very quiet, very still.

The end of the third night came and, as dawn broke, Savitri opened her eyes and knew that this was the day of which the astrologers had spoken. Her heart beating fast, she entered the cottage to sit by her sleeping husband's side. She sat until he awoke. She fetched him water for his bath and set his meal before him, and watched as he prepared to go into the forest, for the day's work.

'Let me come with you,' she said to him unexpectedly, and he was surprised. 'You can't leave my parents here alone, Savitri,' he pointed out to her. 'Who will look after them if we both go?'

But they overheard him and interrupted:

'Take her with you, Satyavan. Never has she wanted anything for herself. Let her have her wish now.'

So he gave in. And as they walked together he was suddenly very glad he had let her come. For there was a happiness that she brought with her wherever she went. He saw how it lit up their path, and made the most commonplace things come alive with a beauty all their own.

In the heart of the forest Satyavan stopped. He chose a tree to cut.

'Sit down, Savitri,' he said gently, 'and amuse yourself while I work.'

Savitri sat on the grass and felt the coolness of the forest around her. The sunshine came dancing through the new leaves and set them glistening. Nesting birds flew in and out of them with little twittering noises. A little way away she could see a mother doe licking her fawn; at the flutter of an eyelid they were alerted and bounded off, their short tails flicking behind them. A peacock twirled, magnificent fantail outspread. All around her was the loveliness of life. Her soul thrilled in answer to it.

But in that same moment the thought came to her, painful as a sword-thrust, that nothing, nothing would be the same for her without Satyavan. And she sat without moving, her hands clasped and her heart reaching out to heaven in an agony of prayer. She listened with every nerve of her being. She could hear the strokes of his axe on the tree trunk—firm, steady, regular, and the minutes went relentlessly by. Suddenly she felt her breath catch in her dry throat. She felt her body tremble. For the strokes of Satyavan's axe . . . there was no mistake, no mistake at all, they were growing weaker, fainter.

She raised wild, fear-stricken eyes as she felt a presence coming. A vast darkness, and yet there was no shadow; a blinding light and yet there was a quivering darkness at the heart of it. A figure advanced. It loomed before her. The blows of the axe upon the tree were very faint now, then suddenly they faltered and stopped. She heard the axe fall to the ground. She saw Satyavan's figure stagger towards her and heard his feeble cry: 'Savitri. I—I—feel ill—I feel strange—I feel I am going to——' she caught him in her arms as he fell.

'There, you will be all right soon,' she whispered. 'Rest for a while.'

But the blood was cold within her. She took his head on her lap. His face was pale as ash and his lips were blue. When she smoothed the hair back from his forehead it was damp. There was a cold sweat on his face. She called his name, once, twice, softly at first. Then her frightened voice tore out of her throat, so that all the forest grew still with fear: 'Satyavan! my husband!' But he was silent, and she saw that his breathing had ceased.

And there before her was the person she had seen advancing. He was very near them now, and she knew that he was Yama, god of justice and truth and death.

34

Their eyes met. He had deep-set, red-rimmed eyes. Hidden in their depths was a wisdom, vast and timeless; wonderfully kind and sad eyes; darkly green. As she looked into them she found she was no more afraid. She felt strangely calm. She saw the rope in his hands and the loop at the end of it, and she recognized it: it was the noose he used for the souls of creatures he must take from the region of the living to the region of the dead. He was testing the strength of the knot. He stooped a little to slip the loop around Satyavan's neck. She raised her hand in protest and he looked at her steadily for a second, as he realized that she could see him. Then he spoke to her:

'It is over, child. Satyavan is dead and I have come to take him to the land of the dead. You have been a brave and good wife, but you must give him up to me, for now he is mine.'

'It is strange that I see you, lord,' Savitri murmured, 'strange that I hear your voice. Could it be a dream?'

'You are not dreaming,' he answered, 'I am real. To ordinary people I am invisible. It needs a fine vision to see heavenly beings. You have acquired that vision by your long days of prayer and fasting and penance. That is why you are able to see me.'

Yama slipped the noose around Satyavan's neck and tightened the knot. He turned round and began to walk, dragging Satyavan after him. Savitri rose. She began to follow him and her husband. Through the forest they went, following the southward course. After a while the forest and the country of the living were left behind, and they were walking over a lonely path, where cold winds blew and all around was a ghostly half-light. Yama's great black buffalo was waiting there for him and followed him as he walked by. As they went on there was a movement in the misty haze. She heard a deep terrible growling and two dogs lifted their snarling savage faces. Their flanks quivered menacingly and they strained at the chains that held them. With a stern word of command to each, Yama stepped into his kingdom, and Savitri, without hesitation or pause, followed after him. The brutes continued to growl. Yama stopped and turned. He saw Savitri.

'Why, what are you doing here, child?' he asked in surprise. 'Following my husband,' she answered him simply. 'Wherever he goes, there I must go too, must I not?' and she looked into his face and smiled at Yama. He shook his head. His green eyes were worried. 'Not into the region of the dead, child.' He smiled gently at her. 'No living person may walk into this region. No one has ever done it.'

'Perhaps,' she agreed, 'but I must be with my husband. I cannot be false to my vow, can I?'

'No person can follow another into death,' Yama explained, 'and Satyavan your husband is dead.' He spoke with a cruel finality but she looked up into his face and said quietly: 'When I married Satyavan, I promised to go with him wherever he went. You, Yama, are the god of truth. Surely you will not want me to be false to my vow?'

'But this is death,' he explained patiently, 'and death is different from life. Death is the end of life and a wall separates the two. Death knows no promises. With death comes the great parting of ways.' But she was unconvinced. 'But I saw no wall, no boundary, as I walked into your kingdom, great god,' she said. 'I saw that death is only a continuation of life.'

He frowned uneasily at her, and there was a flicker of annoyance in his voice as he answered: 'No one has ever argued with me before.'

'Perhaps they are afraid of you,' she suggested.

'And you are not?' he asked, his voice sharp with surprise.

'Oh no,' she smiled. 'I have walked five steps with you and that makes you my friend. I will come with you the whole long journey. Why should I fear you?'

He stared at her. 'Why should you fear me?' he echoed. 'But child, even hardened old warriors shrink when they hear my name. I am *death*, Savitri, *death*! My name is hated and feared. I come riding upon my great black buffalo and drag souls away, leaving behind me great wastes of tears and sorrow!'

He searched her face for signs of fear but there were none. 'Perhaps you only act a part,' she suggested. 'Perhaps you needlessly frighten simple folk.'

He regarded her with mingled surprise and curiosity, realizing suddenly that in her childlike innocence this young and simple girl had seen beyond his grim outward appearance into his innermost heart. But he remembered the work he must do, and thought importantly to himself: 'How can I allow her to move me from the path of my duty? Duty comes first.'

And yet the girl had a charm that set all his defences quivering. He went over a hundred arguments in his mind, but in the end all he could say to her, rather lamely, was, 'You cannot come with me, child, you cannot come with me.'

'But I must,' insisted Savitri, 'I have no choice, you see.'

36

'Your time has not come,' Yama argued, surprised at his own patience. 'Go back, Savitri.'

Then suddenly remembering the weakness that is at the core of every mortal creature, he smiled at her. God-like and gracious, he held out his hands and went on: 'I am pleased with you and I bless you. I will grant you any boon you desire.'

Her eyes sparkled and all her being leaped up as she opened her mouth to speak, but Yama held up his forefinger quickly. 'Any favour, I say, child, except the life of Satyavan. That I cannot give, for that belongs to me.'

Her face fell. 'That is a pity,' she murmured. 'And yet, how good you are, Yama!'

He was flattered despite himself, but would not allow himself to unbend: 'Go on, ask!' he said expansively.

She joined her hands: 'My father-in-law is blind,' she began. 'Grant, kind god, that he may get back his sight.' He was pleased with her request, and pleased with himself for his graciousness. The warmth of his own benevolence and kindness flooded his being: 'Gladly, will I grant you your prayer, Savitri,' he answered her. 'Death has a cruel appearance, but he conceals a kind and generous heart, as you see. Now go home, child, for I must be on my way.' Then he turned and began to walk on.

'Well, that was easy,' he thought. 'I had feared I would never shake her off. But it is fortunate that human creatures can always be swayed by gifts.'

But he sighed a little as he walked. The burden he was carrying seemed heavy, and the way seemed very long. The girl's gentle voice kept returning to him, like an echo. He seemed to see her before him, and the brightness of her smile. And suddenly he felt very dull and old and stale. He felt a vast loneliness at the core of his being and understood that he had always been lonely and never known it until now. For one moment when the girl Savitri had looked into his eyes and smiled, the darkness inside him had lit up, the loneliness was dispelled. Never, though he was a god, had he known such a sweet happiness as the happiness Savitri had brought him that day.

'Well,' he thought wearily. 'All things must come to an end and so too my brief encounter with this child of sunshine.'

As Yama trudged on, he heard light footsteps again, behind him. He stopped and the footsteps stopped. He turned round, and there before him stood Savitri.

'You are walking in the region of the dead!' he exclaimed, agitated.

'Yes, I am,' she nodded earnestly. 'Because wherever my husband goes, there I must go too.' Yama was totally at a loss. 'This—this—' he sputtered, 'this is completely unheard of. Have I not told you that your time has not yet come, and that no one may enter these regions a second before or a second after what is given to him by the gods? Can you not understand that all these things are pre-ordained, that if men did not live by the law the whole order would collapse?' But he knew by the look in her eye that she knew no order or law, but had only her love to guide her. She had no intention of obeying him. He was sorely perplexed. The only thing he could think of was to bribe her again with more gifts.

'Listen Savitri,' he said, 'ask of me anything you like, except the life of Satyavan and then you must go home.'

Her eyes grew thoughtful: 'My parents-in-law live in poverty,' she said. 'Please grant that my father-in-law's kingdom and wealth may be restored to him.'

'Granted, granted!' Yama beamed. 'Now go back, child, and return to the world where you belong,' and he waved his hand in the direction of that world. Then he lifted up Satyavan and put him across the buffalo's back. He gave the animal a push and it raised its big horned head and began to move through the slush.

They had not gone far, however, when Yama realized that Savitri was still following him. Suddenly he lost his temper: how dare she disobey him; how dare she disregard his words. 'Oh!' he thought, 'the *humiliation* of it! To be thwarted by a slip of a girl!' And he gnashed his teeth. In his rage he began to lead her where the sharp-edged stones and thorns drew blood from her feet, where terrible vapours rose around her, threatening to suffocate her. He took her where she began to hear evil voices: 'Go back, go back, this is the country of the dead and no living creature may enter it.'

'But Satyavan,' cried Savitri, 'how can I leave him? I must go where he goes.' And she continued to follow Yama, until at last, weary, desperate, his patience worn thin, the god of death sat down on a rock. She came and stood by him. He noticed how, without knowing it, she stood in a small pool of light. But this time it irritated him to see that light. 'You are a foolish girl,' he told her angrily. 'But I will give you another gift. Yes a gift, any gift except Satyavan's life. Take any gift and go.' He drew himself up to his height and extended his hand.

'How generous you are,' she murmured and then went on: 'Lord, my father has no sons. Give him sons, gracious god!'

38

His heart softened. Did she never think of herself, this brave girl with her gentle voice and her quick, warm smile? All the gifts she asked were for others—nothing, nothing for herself.

He looked curiously at her and then nodded. 'Willingly,' he assented. 'It is a good wish and easy to grant. And now go home child, and great happiness will be yours.' But go she would not. 'I cannot leave Satyavan,' she said and he felt cheated.

'I will teach you what it is to follow me,' he muttered. 'It will be much worse than before. What you have seen so far is nothing to what you will see.' Then he took her over desert wastes and treacherous marshland, across territory where the weeping spirits of people struck down by plague and cholera and the dreaded smallpox roamed; he took her where dead mothers wailed for children left behind, and headless warriors rode on skeleton horses that gleamed white in the murky darkness. They went through streets where murdered men cried out wordlessly for revenge, and others that were loud with the hollow voices of sinners being bled for their sins. She saw hungry spirits and thirsty spirits, the victims of famine, earthquake and flood, and they stretched out their hands to her and pulled at her garments.

They went through hells of fire and hells of ice, and fearful hells where dead men tortured those who had likewise tortured them in their lifetime. She saw death dances and death cults and savage death rites.

'Go, foolish girl, go,' called Yama, and his voice seemed to come to her from a distance. 'Go, or it will be even worse!' But though her face was pale, her eyes were determined. She would not turn back.

Yama tried again. 'People's life-stories are written long before they are born,' he explained to her, 'and what is written can neither be erased nor changed. Fate promised Satyavan to me, Savitri, and no one can challenge fate.'

But she only repeated doggedly: 'How can I leave him, Yama? Satyavan is my husband and, where he goes, I must follow.'

Yama cried out in desperation. 'Take yet another gift, any gift but Satyavan's life, for Satyavan is mine!' And he thought to himself: 'Soon she will weaken, for after all she is only made of mortal flesh.' Yama's emerald eyes looked over the still blue features of the dead man he was taking. His long fingers wound in and out of his hair. As they did so, his confidence in himself began to return, and he smiled with the pride of possession and power. How helpless and thin was this girl Savitri, he was thinking; how foolish and pathetic her

40

childlike faith! 'Well,' said Yama aloud, 'you are a brave girl, Savitri, and I am pleased with you. So this time I will myself bestow a gift on you. And it shall be for you.' As he spoke, his heart began to expand with emotion. Men called him Kritanta, the finisher, Bhimasasana, the one of terrible decrees, and Pretaraja, king of ghosts. 'Ah,' he thought, 'I should have been more rightly named Varada, bestower of gifts, Sukhadayaka, giver of happiness.'

She was kneeling before him. 'A boon, a boon,' he repeated, thrusting out his chest. 'You shall have a boon to remember Yama by. What shall I grant you? How shall I make you happy?' He laughed with pride, and then, his eyes growing kindly, he murmured: 'You shall have great happiness, child.' But she answered nothing and he realized with something of a pang that his gifts meant little to her. Her thoughts were all with Satyavan. 'What might she want? What could I tempt her with?' he wondered. 'Gold? Silver? Rare and precious gems?' But he frowned, muttering: 'No, wealth holds no charms for her.' He toyed with the idea of empire and power, but these too he brushed aside knowing that she did not care for them.

What then?

'What?' Yama repeated aloud and then as an idea flashed across his mind, he snapped his fingers triumphantly: 'I know what it is a woman wants. A woman wants children and the happiness of motherhood.'

He glowed at the thought of his own divine insight.

'Ah,' he sighed. 'How wonderful to be a god; to be able to bestow gifts on people!' Lifting up his hand in a majestic gesture he uttered in a voice, deep and solemn:

'May you experience the joy of motherhood, Savitri; may your children bring you joy.' And he threw back his proud head and closed his eyes in a dream, until a peal of silvery laughter shook him into reality. He looked about him bewildered and confused.

'Yama!' Savitri was laughing. 'Yama! If I am to have children, then surely Satyavan must return to me, must he not? Did I not vow that Satyavan would be the father of my children? You are the god of truth, so who should know that better than you?' Then extending her hands to him, and still laughing, she went on: 'Yama, you have no choice but to remove the noose from his neck and release him.'

He opened his mouth to speak, but so astonished was he that the words would not come. Then something snapped inside him and he found himself laughing. Rich, joyous laughter, bubbling out of hidden depths, making the tears run down his swarthy cheeks. His crown went askew as his big frame shook.

At last, wiping the tears from his face, he replied: 'You are right, Savitri, I see I have no choice except to loosen the knot from his neck, and give him his life.'

After a while he grew graver: 'Never before has such a thing happened,' he said to her, 'Never before has a dead man returned to life!'

That was how Savitri won her husband back from the god of death. One minute she was laughing; the next, her eyes brimmed over with warm, gentle tears she could no longer contain in her heart. Through them she saw Yama restore Satyavan to her. 'My blessings go with you, dear child,' said Yama: His own heart was trembling and he felt tears prickling at the corners of his eyes. It was an unfamiliar sensation. Tears were for human creatures. And he was a god. But he was not sorry for the strange experience.

He saw her small slender form recede as she went farther and farther from him, with Satyavan following like one in a dream. As long as Yama could see them, his eyes followed the pair, and then, when the two small specks had crossed the illusory horizon that separates the world of the dead from the world of the living, he sighed and gave his buffalo a push. Back he went, empty-handed, into his dark and silent kingdom. But the memory of her smile remained with him and the sound of her laughter stayed in his lonely heart.

To Savitri it seemed that hardly a moment had passed before she found herself sitting as before upon the green grass with Satyavan's head on her lap. Nothing had changed, except that the sun was now setting and the shadows were gathering. Satyavan stirred, and she saw, through the tears in her eyes, how colour was returning to his cheeks, life to his limbs. His eyelids fluttered, then opened, and he looked about him dazed. But when his eyes met hers, recognition gathered in them. 'I have—I have had a dream,' he whispered to her, 'such a strange dream, Savitri. I dreamed that a man, a fearful man, was dragging me away, far, far away. I was chained to him and helpless.'

'Do not think about these things,' she answered him. 'You have been asleep and dreaming. And what are dreams after all.'

And her smile was so full of love that he felt strong again.

'We must go,' she reminded him. 'It is late and your parents will be anxious.' She would have helped him up, but he laughed and would take none of her help.

Yama, being the god of truth, kept his promises. Dyumatsena's sight returned. There was a rebellion in his country, the usurper was driven out and Dyumatsena was reinstated. Savitri's mother bore sons and the question of succession was solved.

As for Savitri, happiness walked with her through the days of her life, and Satyavan loved her and considered himself blessed to have her. Their children played happily in the palace gardens.

What more could she want?

'Life is very sweet,' mused Savitri as she watched them, 'but it cannot last for ever.'

And after a while when Yama came for their two souls, hers and Satyavan's, he found them smiling and ready. Willingly she and Satyavan went with him to the region of the dead. Hand in hand they entered it as many years ago they had emerged hand in hand from it into the region of the living.

43

3

The Two Demon Brothers

I

There was a strange silence over all the earth. The very leaves and blades of grass were still. The birds fluttered soundless in the air and the animals sat huddled in their dens and caves. The sea held its breath.

Two little gods peered out from heaven's shining windows, wondering about the cause of this unnatural silence. What they saw made them tremble. Frightened, they came running to the court of the king of gods, Indra, where he sat among the heavenly beings, and there, breathless and pale-faced, they related what they had seen.

'The asura brothers,' they panted, 'are deep in prayer and all the universe trembles before the power of their meditation.' The gods, who, till then had been lolling back on silken cushions and golden thrones, sat up wide awake and alert.

'Hiranyaksha and Hiranyakashipu, twin brothers and rulers of asura-land, have determined to conquer the universe,' said the godlings, 'and so great is the power of their meditation that the earth is silent and people are stricken with fear.'

The listening gods turned in alarm to their king and leader Indra, hoping to draw courage from him, but Indra's teeth were chattering and his knees knocking together in fear. 'It seems that our end is near,' wailed the thirty-three crore gods. 'Who can tell what will happen and whose downfall the demons will bring about?'

And it was at that very moment that laughter sounded—laughter that shook the mountains and made the heavens shudder. The gods hid their faces in terror: it was the laughter of the asura brothers.

Far down below, in the world of the demons, the brothers had opened their eyes after long years of deep meditation and prayer. And when they did so the universe lit up. The asuras looked around them, and the birds twittered and sang. They stood up, and life on earth began to move again. They laughed, and mortal creatures clung to each other in fear.

Their laughter was terrible. It echoed and re-echoed in every corner of the universe. The skies seemed to tear open at the sound. They laughed remembering their past: their birth and the signs that accompanied it—how the sun's face had clouded over and how a fiery red darkness had licked the moon's face; how violent winds had rocked the mountains and lashed at the oceans. They laughed remembering how their minds and bodies had grown powerful and strong with each day. They remembered the restlessness and wildness of their boyhood, as they wandered over hill and dale, free as the birds of the air; they laughed remembering how their fame had spread, and how their asura subjects fell on their knees in awe before them and worshipped them.

45

It was only in the silence of the night, as they lay under the stars, that their minds had travelled in other directions. Then, in the stillness, they wondered about the mystery at the heart of all creation. They wondered about the very beginning of all things, the source, the first seed . . . and a voice seemed to whisper to them: 'You and you alone are the beginning and you are the end. You are all things and all things are in you.'

Then strange things happened to them. The universe seemed to fall away about them; there arose everywhere the mighty sound of Om, the first sound that ever was, the sound that accompanied creation. Their bodies seemed to be no more; their minds ceased to be. The sense of separateness left them and they became one with all things.

When the attendants came in the morning bringing them water in jewelled pitchers to wash, the boys were in a trance. Their bodies were rigid, their eyes closed, and they were lost to the world. The frightened servants fell on their knees before them in worship and touched their heads to the ground. But the trance passed. When the demon brothers opened their eyes there was nothing left of the experience they had gone through, except the energy that remained with them. They longed for the experience to repeat itself, for the peace and joy it brought, but they saw only the gibbering, quaking servants kneeling before them crying out that they were gods.

'The Gods . . .?' laughed the brothers, 'Those puny, little feeble-minded creatures who live in heaven? Know and understand, fools, that we are infinitely more than gods—infinitely greater, infinitely wiser, infinitely more powerful.'

They stood up. They shouted with laughter and swinging their maces about, they stepped out of their palace and beyond its walls. They went striding over the lands of neighbouring people, making war and conquering one territory after another. They made captives of kings and princes and yoked them to their ploughs, and they seized their womenfolk and carried them away.

'We are the lords of the universe and we shall rule for ever,' they said, puffing out their chests.

'Of that, asuras, there is some doubt!'

The demon brothers swung round fiercely at the mocking voice. Who was it that challenged them? But anger gave place to surprise when they saw before them only a small, insignificant-looking person who looked rather like a wandering beggar, a street-singer. His clothes were ochre-dyed. There was a sound of music all round him as he strummed with his deft, light fingers upon a simple lute. The air was flower-scented where he walked, and there were garlands of flowers on his neck and wrists. He had merry twinkling eyes and a dimpled smile. Who was he? A heavenly being? Had they not seen him before?

'Perhaps you have and perhaps you haven't,' he said, answering their unspoken thoughts. 'You see, I am Narada . . . .' and his eyes sparkled with hidden laughter.

'The mischief-maker!' the brothers were about to say, but Narada interrupted them, speaking in a breathless, hurried way: 'You are very powerful, asura brothers, yes, but as to your dream of ruling forever . . .' he paused and looked very doubtful, 'well, I am not so sure . . . .' And he played on the instrument, a few quick and lovely notes. 'You see, mighty ones,' he went on, before the brothers could interrupt him, 'however strong and rich and powerful you may be, there is one enemy you will never conquer. You have forgotten death, my friends, you have forgotten death! Death is the one enemy you will never conquer! Whatever wealth and territory you might acquire, however learned you may become, whatever enemies you might overcome and subdue, death will one day defeat you and lay you low!'

And he strummed away on his lute and seemed preoccupied with other things. The brothers did not notice the sidelong glances that he cast upon them.

'Idler!' they roared at him. 'Wastrel and vagabond—go from here. We have no time for you.'

Narada slipped away as noiselessly as he had come. But the sound

46

of his music lingered after him, with the fragrance of his flowers. And his words hung in the air: 'Death is the one enemy you will never conquer. Whatever you do, death will one day defeat you.'

The brothers tried to dismiss their meeting with him as a dream, but deep in their hearts something had raised its head—a small chill pinpoint of fear! Never before had they known fear. But now, wherever they went, it went with them, and it spoke in the echoes of Narada's voice, softly, mockingly.

'Death,' the brothers whispered to each other at last, 'then it is death that must be conquered. We must be deathless and everlasting!'

When they realized this, they knew what they must do.

In their heavens the gods began to breathe a little easier.

One day the asura brothers left empire and wealth in the hands of their ministers and, dressed in clothes of bark, began to wander, seeking the answer to death. But no one had it, and wherever they went, their fear followed them, and they seemed to see death's leering face and to hear its mocking voice. So the brothers decided to approach Shiva, god of destruction. They retired into the heart of the forest and there, set their hearts on him. Ceaselessly they prayed for many days, and such was the power of their prayer, that once more the gods began to quake, and to wring their hands, sobbing: 'We are ruined, done for; all is over with us.'

The asura brothers prayed on, until at last Shiva appeared before them, standing before their eyes in tiger-skin and matted locks, the serpent around his blue neck and the crescent moon over his temple. The sight left them breathless and speechless. Perhaps they might never have remembered to ask a boon, had not Shiva himself reminded them.

Then the brothers, swelling with pride, demanded from Shiva the power to conquer death.

'Conquer death?' echoed Shiva, eyebrows raised in surprise. 'Do you not know, good friends, that no one has yet conquered death? All things that are born must die. This is nature's law, and even I, a god, must live by nature's law. I too must one day die. How can I grant you immortality?'

The asuras were astonished. Was the god they thought so powerful, only a weakling after all? Had all their meditations been for nothing?

'What shall we do then?' they demanded angrily. 'To whom shall we go?'

'Well,' murmured Shiva, 'perhaps you could try Brahma, and

perhaps he may help you.'

Disappointed, the brothers started on their meditation and penance all over again, until four-faced Brahma appeared before them to ask what they wanted. But when they named their wish, Brahma was amused.

'Why, you ask for the impossible!' he exclaimed, his eight eyes twinkling, 'for I am powerless against death; though I am the creator, I was myself created, and like all creation, I too must end one day. How can I help you?'

'Is there no one then that can grant us power over death?' cried

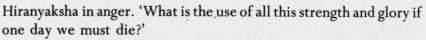

Hiranyaksha in anger. 'What is the use of all this strength and glory if one day we must die?'

'That is how it is,' Brahma answered rather helplessly. 'Surely,' cried the asuras through clenched teeth, 'surely there must be some way. Can you not show us some way?'

'Well,' began Brahma, but he spoke reluctantly, 'you could go to Vishnu. Vishnu was never born, nor will he ever die. Vishnu was and is and will forever be. He may be able to help you.' And so they prayed to Vishnu.

'Escape death?' echoed Vishnu appearing before them, at the end of their meditation and prayer. 'But death, my friends, is supreme!'

But this time the brothers were determined that their efforts should not go in vain. They refused to move from this spot and clung to Vishnu's feet, insisting on his blessing.

'Ask any other boon except this one,' Vishnu begged them. 'It will be granted.' Hiranyaksha thought for a while.

Some way must be found . . . some trick . . . some ruse by which Vishnu could be outwitted into granting him immortality. 'Listen Vishnu,' he began at last, and there was a cunning little smile on his lips. 'It is true that one day I will die, but grant that nothing

will kill me—neither disease nor weapon, nor the forces of nature. Grant that neither human creature nor demon, nor beast nor bird nor insect nor reptile nor fish may kill me.' And he went on to enumerate, to count on his fingers, to count with the hairs of his head the names of all the gods who lived in the heavens and all the men who lived on the earth, and every demon who dwelt in the underworld, saying: 'Such and such shall not be the cause of my death.'

Vishnu agreed to all he said, listening patiently, making no attempt to contradict or interrupt. Hiranyaksha went on and on;

listing the weapons and poisons and forces of nature that could kill; he named animals and reptiles and insects and birds. He mentioned each one, begging Vishnu that he make it powerless against him.

'Yes,' agreed Vishnu as each was named, 'it shall not be the cause of your death, asura.'

Hiranyaksha went on with his enumeration. He named the biggest and the smallest creatures, and the years went by as he spoke. At the end of the narration, Vishnu said: 'Is that all? Have you mentioned every creature?'

'Yes, I have!' laughed the demon, 'I have mentioned every human being and god and demon, every animal, bird, insect and reptile. Vishnu, grant that none of these may be the cause of my death and I shall be satisfied.'

'Granted,' smiled Vishnu, raising his hand in blessing, and the asura went back to his kingdom, roaring with laughter. 'I have fooled Vishnu,' he gloated, 'I have tricked him into making me immortal.'

Now that the fear of death was gone, there remained no limits to Hiranyaksha's ambition and pride. Over land and sea he went, reckless and without thought or mercy, cutting down all who stood in his way.

'Death will not touch me now,' he laughed, 'I have outwitted Vishnu and have nothing to fear.'

So he went all over the seven worlds till the day came when he confronted Indra himself and made him kneel before him. He ruled without mercy or law and the people groaned under his tyranny. They cried out to the gods but the gods were helpless. Then, in their despair, the people remembered Vishnu and prayed to him. Vishnu, reclining upon his serpent throne, opened his eyes, knowing that the time was approaching when he must take birth again to save the good and destroy evil.

It came one fearful day when Hiranyaksha's eyes fell on Prithvi, the earth goddess, and beloved wife of Vishnu. He saw her in a woodland grove and held his breath at her loveliness. He wanted to possess her, but she fled from him when he called her. He was astounded. He had never been thwarted before. His desire became a passion and, staring about him with crazed eyes, he felt that nothing would be of any consequence or worth if he did not capture her and make her his own. Tormented by the memory of her, he saw her lovely face wherever he went—in waving fields of golden corn, in forest and ocean, brook and rivulet, wild flower and grass, hill and

50

valley, city and village.

'Who is she?' he demanded. And when he heard the answer, he laughed.

'Why, if she is Vishnu's, then I have every right to claim her, for I am greater than Vishnu, greater than all the gods. Bring her to me.'

The servants shrank away in fear, protesting and pleading that they dared not commit so heinous a crime as lay their hands on a goddess. The bravest of his ministers and counsellors came to him, begging him to listen to reason, but the asura shouted at them in anger: 'You are chicken-livered cowards, all of you! Afraid of that sleepy-eyed youth and his four arms! Go, go back to the safety of your little homes, and I will bring her myself. I fear no one. I have conquered everything and everyone—even death.'

Then he went up a mountain and standing on its peak he called out to the goddess in a thunderous voice, 'Come to me, Prithvi, for I have power and strength and wealth such as Vishnu never saw in all his life. What is Vishnu but a smooth-skinned weakling who does nothing but sleep and dream all day upon a ridiculous snake throne that floats on a sea of milk . . . .' and his loud laughter filled the mountains and valleys.

'Vishnu sleeps,' he said, 'and while he sleeps, I have conquered all this and made it mine. Do you see, Prithvi, earth goddess? I am greater than Vishnu. Come to me then, for all this I will share with you. I shall seat you on my throne and make you my queen.'

But there was no answer to his call, and the empty echoes of his voice, reverberating from hill to hill, came mocking him in his solitude. A streak of light shot through the thicket of trees. And he started. He was sure he saw her, then unsure again. Was it only the fish leaping in the sun-dappled brook; or the brightness of a kingfisher's wing? Or was it a dewdrop glinting? His blood sang at the thought of possessing her, and he began to run about searching desperately for her. He knew she must be there somewhere within reach, and it puzzled him that she did not come running at his call. Why did she not come? Why?

Suddenly for the first time in his life he felt a sense of humiliation; of defeat. He swore in a terrible voice that he would not rest or sleep or eat or drink until he had captured this goddess and made her his. Even as he thought this, he saw her flying through the forest, her face white with fear. He lunged forward to catch her, but she vanished like lightning. He was left standing, with only empty air clutched in his great fists and nothing but the faint elusive perfume of spring flowers in the space through which she had passed.

In a fury he began to run again. 'I must have her,' he sobbed. 'I will get her, possess her, enslave her, and then she will know what it is to cross me!'

He ran about like a mad creature. He did not care that his clothes were torn in thorn bushes, that his skin bled; that his face and body were spattered with mud and filth. Blind with desire, seeing nothing but the form of the lovely goddess before him, Hiranyaksha could not see the terrible omens and signs that came out of the heavens

above, neither the comets in the sky nor the darkness that covered the face of the sun and the moon, nor the screaming forms of the planets that changed their course in terror and whirled in drunken circles through space. Deaf to reason, he did not hear the voices of friends who begged him not to defy heaven; nor did he hear the fearful braying of asses and the screeching of owls, evil sounds that warned him of the disasters and calamities that lay before him. His burning eyes saw nothing but Prithvi's fleeing form and he pursued her over the whole earth, crying out to her to come, to surrender to him.

When he had pursued her for long, dreary months, he realized, one day, that she was weakening. He was drawing near—she could not run much farther or much longer. The knowledge brought him no joy, only a black anger, and a savage desire for revenge. It hammered at the walls of his skull as he caught her at last and heard her anguished scream: 'Vishnu! Lord of heaven and earth!'

'Vishnu!' he panted, bending over her, menacingly close. 'I tell you, fool, Vishnu is nothing before me . . . nothing . . . .' But she continued to moan and call Vishnu's name.

He seized her by the hair: 'You are mine,' he cried in a strangled voice. 'You are in my power.'

53

Then, deaf to her screams and her desperate entreaties, he dragged her with him, over desert sands and rugged wastes, until, one dark night, he reached the ocean and stepped into the waves, taking her after him. Outside, the stars rained blood and fire and the whole universe shuddered. Down through the green ocean he went, taking her with him, and the water creatures glided away in fear. He went deeper and deeper still until he reached at last the asura kingdom, and knew his journey had ended. Within him his heart was like stone, cold and hard. They entered the gold-domed palace and, at the sight of it, his spirits revived. In a sudden burst of elation he cried out to her:

'See, lovely one, lift up your head and see the shining splendour that will surround you, if you will only agree to be mine.'

But she she recoiled from him, hissing curses like an angry snake, until in desperation he ordered her to be chained and imprisoned. He heard her cries as he lay in his lonely bed, sleepless, and in torment.

'Vishnu, beloved, deliver me . . . . Vishnu, Vishnu . . . .'

Upon his serpent throne where it floated in the timeless, changeless milk-sea of eternity, Vishnu stirred and smiled as he heard Prithvi's call. Then before his own eyes, he saw himself take a new form and birth. Of his breath was formed a minute particle, smaller, infinitely smaller than a mote. Vishnu looked on. He saw it spin in the air, take shape and grow with every second, until it became a mighty tusked boar that shone with the light of a thousand suns. He saw it go through space and descend upon the earth. The people looked up at the dazzling light and heard his dreadful cry: 'I am Varaha, the heavenly boar, incarnation of Vishnu,' and hearing it, they wept with joy, realizing that they would be free at last.

Hiranyaksha sat on his throne and Prithvi stood before him in chains. She was very pale. Her dishevelled hair fell over her tear-wet face. And yet she was beautiful. His eyes drank in her beauty and he felt his head swimming. He stretched out his arms: 'You will have everything,' he pleaded with her again, 'Only give up Vishnu, and all I have will be yours . . . .'

He beckoned to his attendants: 'Bring her to me. I will lift her on to my lap.' At his words a shudder went through the hall and the carved rafters shook. The servants stared stupidly at him, unable to grasp the meaning of his words and, as they realized that he meant what he said, they reeled before the enormity of the sin he contemplated. 'Cowards!' he yelled. 'Fools and cowards. I . . . .' But he never completed even the thought of that sin. For, at that moment, he felt the ground under his throne rock violently, while from outside came a mighty voice that shook heaven and earth.

'Hiranyaksha, prepare to meet your death, for the hour has come!' He looked about him and saw how his courtiers and attendants trembled, their eyes filled with fear. Why did they tremble so? Why were his own hands shaking? To steady them he clutched at the arms of his throne and the spasm of fear passed. He laughed, recognizing the long-forgotten voice, then cried out: '*Death*, Vishnu? . . . death did you say? And have you forgotten that for me there is no death, no end? Did you not grant me the blessing of immortality . . . long, long years ago?'

'Hiranyaksha,' Varaha's voice rang out like a mighty gong, 'give up Prithvi. Beg her pardon; your sins will be forgiven you.'

'Sin?' roared the asura. 'You dare to talk to me of sin, Vishnu . . . that little bugbear that the gods invented to frighten timid mortals into obedience and good behaviour! What have I to do with sin . . . I who have conquered the earth and humbled the pride of the gods? Understand that I am above sin—above good, above evil. Go back to your snake-bed to sleep and dream, for I will never give up Prithvi, never! I will fight for her and I will win, for no one and nothing can vanquish me . . . . This was your own promise to me.'

The earth groaned and trembled. His throne swayed. The lamps flickered and went out. And all was darkness. The asura stood up and the echoes of Varaha's voice resounded from every corner: 'Do not be so sure, Hiranyaksha.' But Hiranyaksha was already walking towards the voice. There was a savage drumming in his blood, to the words of a wild primitive chant: 'Nothing, nothing can harm me. Nothing can bring about my death. No human creature, no god, no asura. No force of nature can touch me, no weapon be of any avail. For I am deathless. I am immortal. As for animals, have I not named every creature and obtained from you, Vishnu, the promise that it shall not be the cause of my death? . . . Have I not . . . .' And then he stopped suddenly and stared into the face of the boar. Its tusks gleamed in the darkness, and he could see the glint of the small black eyes above the snout. Icy fingers clutched at his heart and in a flash he knew that fate had been cleverer than he . . . that fate was laughing at him because he had made a mistake . . . one small slip of his colossal memory, and he had forgotten to name the boar! The drums within him ceased for a second. Then the rhythm changed:

'Death has caught up with you at last, death . . . death . . . . death . . . .' He stood there paralysed staring into the tusked boar's face. Then anger surged through him. He raised his mace above his head and with a fearful yell he charged.

'Though I have been cheated, I will fight you still, Vishnu, Varaha, whoever you may be!' he bellowed, and the fearful death dance began—the duel between Hiranyaksha the asura, and Varaha the boar. The frightened planets raced across space, the earth split open and all the heavens shook. They fought many rounds and, at the end of each, Hiranyaksha felt the strength ebbing from his body. But he would not yield. As often as Varaha threw him upon the ground he sprang up again, bleeding, bruised, torn, broken and fighting for his life. But against death no man can win, and in the end, Varaha the boar rushed at the asura in one final lunge and gored him with his tusk until he fell bleeding to the ground. Once, twice, three times he tried to raise himself up but the strength was gone from him, and it was all he could do to gasp out:

'You promised me immortality, Vishnu. Is this the way you honour your promise?'

Varaha loomed above him, bloody and terrible: 'I promised that the animals and things you enumerated should not bring about your death,' he reminded him. 'You were clever, Hiranyaksha, but not as clever as you thought. Your mind slipped; your memory made an error and in that error lay the seed of your destiny.'

'Well, you are cleverer than I, Vishnu,' sighed Hiranyaksha wearily. His voice was feeble now and death was very near. Then his eyes lit up. 'Nevertheless,' he gasped, 'nevertheless, Vishnu, I have won.'

'How?' asked Varaha.

'Because, as I lie dying I see in you the face of god, and he who sees the face of god shall be immortal even if his body should be reduced to death.'

His blood-drenched body twitched and convulsed, but his lips were smiling, and his eyes glowed like live embers. 'I regret nothing,' he whispered, 'nothing, Vishnu. I am above sin and above good. I am beyond pleasure and beyond pain. I am happy. I am at peace.'

And after that he spoke no more. His body twitched once and then lay still, stretched out upon the blood-soaked earth like a great tree felled in the forest by the wood-cutter's axe.

The small creatures who inhabited the earth and the heavenly regions saw a dazzling comet streak across space and light up all the universe with its brilliance.

'It is the asura's spirit,' they whispered. 'It is his dauntless, unvanquished, limitless spirit, that knows no end, no decay, no death.' For a while they stood in awed and hushed silence. And then they went about their little humdrum tasks and forgot what they had seen.

There was blood on Varaha's face and on his snout, as he entered the dungeons where Prithvi languished. His tusks gleamed red. She rose at the sight of him, weeping and laughing at the same time, crazed with joy. She was small, and fragile, incredibly beautiful. Very gently, very tenderly Varaha lifted her up in the hollow of his

mighty hand. He placed her upon his blood-stained snout. And then he rose with her upward and earthward, leaving far behind them the mournful chanting of the asuras as they walked in sorrow around their mighty ruler's corpse.

II

News of his brother's death at the hands of Varaha reached Hiranyakashipu in his palace, and when he heard it, he howled with grief. 'Gored to death by a boar!' he wept. 'Hiranyaksha who was so mighty in war, who had conquered the seven worlds and humbled Indra's pride—killed by a wild pig!' No one and nothing could comfort him and, as he lit the funeral pyre, he cried out: 'What use is anything, what use, if this is to be the end?'

Presently, however, he sat up. He felt his spirit reviving. He found himself going over and over again the tragedy of his brother's death.

'It is Vishnu who has done this,' a voice inside him whispered. 'That mischief-maker, that four-armed, lotus-eyed god is at the bottom of it all. Beneath his seemingly innocent eyes, he schemes and plots. Beneath his gentle smile he hides his power and cunning. Vishnu is a betrayer of promises.'

Hiranyakashipu remembered how, many years ago, he too, like his brother, had prayed to Vishnu and begged from him the blessing of immortality. Memories passed through his mind, and he felt the air stir as there came wafting towards him the delicate scent of jasmine and sandal; and faint sounds of music—a soft little melody, plaintive and sweet; a tiny click and clash of cymbals. And then, Narada was before him.

The minstrel's usually cheerful face was serious now, his eyes grave. Hiranyakashipu started. And Narada began to speak:

58

'Do you remember,' murmured Narada, 'that day, many years ago, when you prayed to Vishnu for immortality, and he appeared before you?'

As Narada spoke, that scene of long ago rose up before Hiranyakashipu's eyes: 'You have meditated for many years, Hiranyakashipu,' Vishnu had said to him with his hand raised to bless him. 'And now you may choose the boon you wish me to grant you.'

But when Hiranyakashipu had demanded immortality, Vishnu

had told him that that was one gift he could not grant. For no one, not even the gods, could live forever.

'Ask any other gift or gifts,' Vishnu had said, but Hiranyakashipu had determined to wrest this boon alone, and no other from him. It was the only thing he craved—victory over death. So he had gone on with a crafty look in his eyes: 'Well, Vishnu, if I cannot be immortal, then grant that I do not die in the daytime.' To which Vishnu had answered: 'So be it.'

'And let me not die at night,' Hiranyakashipu had continued. 'Let not death come to me from any weapon, neither sword nor mace, nor dagger nor arrow. Let neither human being nor creature from the animal world be the cause of my death.' Vishnu had blessed him accordingly.

Then Hiranyakashipu had sprung up and laughed saying: 'Ah Vishnu, I have tricked you. You have made me immortal. Death will never touch me now,' at which Vishnu had smiled his gentle smile.

The music of Narada's lute brought back that smile to Hiranyakashipu. It was a mysterious, haunting smile. As he thought of that smile a gloom filled him—a sense of approaching evil. But he roused himself with an effort. His brother's end had been tragic, yes, but he could not mourn forever. At this point Narada's music grew louder and the cymbals made a merry sound. Hiranyaksha was dead, of course, but his empire was there still—a vast empire, green and fruitful, and it was all his now to rule over. He would carry on his brother's name . . . . Narada's music rippled through the air and broke into lovely melodies. As the minstrel sang, new hopes were born in Hiranyakashipu's soul. He remembered that his queen would soon bear him a child. 'Perhaps it will be a boy,' sang Narada to the sound of the one-stringed lute, and the jasmine scent grew strong and heady about him. But when Hiranyakashipu peered to look closely, Narada was not there. Instead messengers were standing before him with the news that a son had been born to his wife. Then, for the first time since his brother's death, new hope filled Hiranyakashipu's heart. He ordered the city to be illuminated, gifts to be distributed to the poor, and prisoners to be released so that all might share his rejoicing.

Later he held the little one in his arms and marvelled to see the perfection of his limbs and the intelligence in his eyes. The sight of the child, the very thought of him, filled him with pride and a sense of power. He named the child Prahlada, and carried him proudly to the great audience hall where the throne stood.

In the centre of that hall was a mighty carved pillar. The pillar was the centre of his great, domed palace, the centre of the vast demon empire itself. It held up the roof of that ancient structure. It was intricately carved, and people marvelled to see its size and strength. It seemed like a symbol of the power and might of the asura empire, its invincibility—all its history and its past, its stirring present and its glorious future. Pride surged through Hiranyakashipu, and he held Prahlada close and whispered: 'You are my pillar and my hope. You are the fulfilment of my dreams. Together we shall reign and our days shall last forever.'

But as he spoke, the memory of his brother's death returned to him, and his face darkened: 'Together we shall defeat that betrayer of promises, that deceiver of men, Vishnu, and bring him to dust. Together we shall be gods and men shall worship us.'

The asura king threw himself with renewed vigour into the affairs of state. There was work to be done. He issued orders that his subjects should cease to worship Vishnu, that Vishnu's temples be broken and the name of Vishnu be removed from every book. He ordered that men worship *him*, Hiranyakashipu, and no other god but him. The people, afraid of being thrown into his torture chambers if they refused, bowed down to him and worshipped him.

60

No one dared to utter aloud the name of Vishnu, the preserver. But there was one person in the palace who would not give up the worship of Vishnu, and that was the queen—Hiranyakashipu's wife and the mother of Prahlada. Vishnu's name was on her lips constantly. She sang it as she nursed her little son and played with him, so that the first words the child, Prahlada, learnt to lisp were the names of Vishnu!

'This,' said the angry Hiranyakashipu, 'is intolerable! Unheard of!' He ordered his wife to give up the worship of Vishnu, and imprisoned her when she disregarded his word. He took her baby

away from her and put him in the care of paid nurses who were obedient to him. So Prahlada grew up in the palace, visiting his mother only once a day in her prison-room.

The nurses tried to teach him to worship his father, but the little boy would shake his head and slip away from them and lead them into merry games of hide-and-seek and chase. His laughter echoed through the palace halls and at its sound they would forget all about Hiranyakashipu's stern orders. It was only when they took him to his mother that they would remember again and worry. For, though the gentle queen never attempted directly to teach the child about Vishnu or to worship him, there was all around her such an atmosphere of holy worship, that the very air seemed to be full of prayer.

The attendants grew uneasy. Hiranyakashipu was uneasy too. He was glad when Prahlada reached the school-going age, for now he could remove him from the women's apartments and the influence of his mother. He sent for Shukra, ancient teacher of the asuras, and commanded him to teach the boy.

He was to teach him mathematics and language, geography, history and statecraft; but above all he was to teach him the great philosophy that there was no god but the self; that all other gods including Vishnu were false; that the self alone was to be worshipped and that the self resided in Hiranyakshipu, conqueror of the seven worlds.

Shukra gladly agreed to take on the lad. Little did he know the stuff Prahlada was made of.

On the very first morning there came a surprise for the old teacher: trouble started when the boys assembled to sing the morning prayer. It was a prayer to king and country. It praised Hiranyakashipu's name in rich, glowing language and glorified the kingdom he ruled over. The king had ordered that it be sung in every school in the land. Shukra had taught the prayer to the pupils and they had learnt it well. He felt a thrill of pride to see and hear them. Then he looked at Prahlada who stood among them like the sun among all the lesser stars. Prahlada was listening with great attention. When Prahlada sang this song, thought Shukra, the king would surely reward the teacher. Shukra nodded encouragement. Prahlada joined in. His voice was clear and lovely. The others fell silent as they listened. Shukra smiled, nodded, smiled again.

Then suddenly he frowned. He jerked his head up and shot a look at the singer with his one eye. What was he singing? He strained his ears to listen more carefully; and as he did so, he shook his head in amazed disbelief . . . . Shukra could not believe his ears. Prahlada sang to *Vishnu*, praising that forbidden god and glorifying his name. Prahlada, utterly oblivious of what was happening, seemed to have become one with the song. A wave of fear swept over the teacher. He called out, but the boy did not hear him. His eyes were closed and it was not till the end of the song that he opened them and smiled at the teacher. The smile seemed to go straight to the old man's dry and withered heart. 'The prince is still a child,' thought Shukra. 'His foolish mother's milk still flows in his veins. But he can be taught and trained. His mind can be influenced and moulded.' He

smiled back very kindly.

'What is this song you are singing, my child?' the one-eyed teacher asked, and Prahlada replied: 'It is the song of Vishnu, a prayer to the lotus-eyed god. It is a song I always sing because it is so beautiful.'

'Where did you learn it?' enquired the schoolmaster. Prahlada's eyes grew thoughtful with the effort to remember: 'Why, I am sure I don't know,' he confessed. 'But I hear it around me all the time.'

'Nonsense!' said the old schoolteacher, frowning. 'These are idle fancies, my child; you are growing up now and must give up your childish play.' He made the boys sit cross-legged around him and began the day's lesson. But things continued to go wrong. Prahlada seemed completely wrapped up in his rebellious thoughts and all that was taught, all that was done, only made him think of Vishnu whom the king, Hiranyakashipu, so vehemently denied. In the numbers of arithmetic Prahlada saw the infinity that was Vishnu, and in the circles and triangles of geometry he saw the beauty of shape and design that was Vishnu's handiwork; in science and geography he saw the wonders of god's creation and in human history he saw Vishnu's mighty plan!

'You must not say that word,' the teacher told him patiently and politely. He dared not speak otherwise than politely, for Prahlada was the king's son. 'The law of the land forbids you to utter that name.'

Prahlada answered in surprise: 'But it is the only word that has meaning. Isn't it Vishnu who makes the sun and stars shine, who gives us life and intelligence? Isn't it Vishnu who lives in all things . . . .'

'Do you argue with a teacher?' snapped Shukra, suddenly annoyed. 'Have you no sense of respect or reverence?'

'Indeed I have, sir,' Prahlada spoke very respectfully. 'I did not mean to argue . . . .'

'You seem to be trying to teach *me*, your teacher,' Shukra broke in testily. He did not like the boy's attitude at all. He felt Prahlada was challenging his authority. He grew very stern and said: 'I am teacher here, not you!' Prahlada nodded and acknowledged this. But when the lesson began again, Shukra noticed that the boy's mind could not be drawn away from Vishnu. Shukra looked at the other pupils. Their lips were moving as they chanted in unison. Their eyes were drowsy and lustreless.

Their faces showed no joy as they repeated mechanically at the beginning and end and in the middle of every lesson: 'Mighty is our ruler Hiranyakashipu, infinite is his power. He shall live and rule the universe forever and his word is truth.'

So they went on chanting. But Prahlada would not join them, and after he had heard them for a few minutes he broke in again and again: 'But it is Vishnu who is above all rulers. It is Vishnu whose power is infinite, who rules the universe and will continue to rule it for ever and ever. Vishnu is truth!'

The other pupils stared dumbfounded at him. Then something began to happen: it was as if a strong current was stirring them. They who had been till then sitting like clods of clay, began to shift in their seats. Shukra, watching anxiously, saw eyelids flicker, mouths twitch, eyebrows lift. Here and there he heard the sound of a swift in-drawn breath. He saw their eyes shine with a new enthusiasm as they looked at Prahlada. Shukra felt very uncomfortable. He did not like it at all. Prahlada was drawing his pupils away from him. The old teacher felt as if the ground under him was suddenly beginning to wobble. He did not know what to do. He was a servant of the king. He depended for his bread upon the king. And he must keep order and see that the king's word was respected. If Prahlada taught them to question it then, he, Shukra, might be held responsible and might even lose his position.

Then, where would he go . . . what would happen to him? He tried to cajole Prahlada and to direct his attention. He offered him prizes and honours if he would give up singing this song of Vishnu; he flattered him and praised his intelligence and ability. But it was of no use at all. Prahlada continued to be respectful and polite; continued to work diligently; but when it came to repeating the king's name and glorifying it, Prahlada would not fall in line! Shukra wrung his hands and was at his wits' end. He saw how Prahlada led the boys in games and play, answered their questions and cleared their doubts; he saw how they looked up to him and loved him. He decided to act before it was too late, and he separated Prahlada from the others in the classroom. But to his dismay the old teacher discovered that the damage had already been done.

Already Prahlada's words had set the boys thinking and questioning. What was more, there was in Prahlada's very presence a strange quality that seemed to quicken and electrify even the air around him. The boys moved towards him as if drawn by some hidden, magnetic power and Shukra could not hold them back. They crowded round him and learned his songs, heard the stories he told;

64

they even began to repeat the forbidden name of Vishnu—at first, timidly and waveringly, and then, gaining courage, they began to sing it joyfully aloud and dance to the lilting tune. Shukra tore his hair in desperation. At times he pleaded with Prahlada; at times scolded and punished him. He caned the boys, cuffed their ears and gagged them in order to silence them. But for all the good it did, he might have tried to hold the sun from shining or the waves of the sea from rolling. At last Shukra appealed to the highest authority, the king himself. Prahlada had to be punished and, because he was the crown prince, Shukra could not touch him.

White-faced and trembling, Shukra stood before Hiranyakashipu and broke the news to him that there was a trouble-brewer, a breaker of the law, a heretic and mischief-maker in their midst.

Hiranyakashipu listened intently. Not a muscle moved in his face. But Shukra saw how his eyes were changing to a fierce red. Tears rolled down Shukra's face.

'I am not to blame, sir, believe me, I am not to blame,' he cried piteously, clasping his hands together. Hiranyakashipu's answer came like the lash of a whip: 'Fool! Are you so weak and foolish that you cannot control one young pupil? What kind of a schoolteacher are you?'

'Sir,' moaned Shukra, 'I have tried everything; but this boy is not like any other. He is not afraid of anything or anybody.'

'Age has made you foolish and weak,' Hiranyakashipu's voice thundered. 'You deserve to be removed from office. Since you are so incompetent and helpless I shall deal with this myself. What is this boy's name? My officer will bring him to me.'

Then shaking in every limb, the teacher told Hiranyakashipu that it was Prahlada, his own son, who was causing the trouble.

Hiranyakashipu was staggered at the news. For a second he turned deathly pale; then a hot anger flushed his face and set his veins throbbing.

'It cannot be!' he shouted. 'You are lying, you traitor . . . you wicked old man—you are telling a lie.'

He clenched his hands, muttering fiercely to himself, and sat back heavily on his throne. And the miserable schoolteacher saw how the giant controlled himself with a tremendous effort of his indomitable will.

'Go,' said Hiranyakashipu at last, 'since you have proved yourself so useless, I will come to the school and deal with this myself. Get out of my sight!' And Shukra hurried away, glad to put as much distance as he could between himself and the angry king.

As Hiranyakashipu approached the schoolhouse he heard the joyful sound of singing. He frowned at the unfamiliar song.

'What is that song they are singing?' he demanded, and bit his lip angrily when Shukra explained, with tears in his eyes and many protestations of his own innocence, that it was the forbidden song of Vishnu.

'Leave off singing that song!' roared Hiranyakashipu standing in the doorway.

His eyes were afire. His voice was like thunder. He towered above them all, and at his command, the boys' voices wavered and their singing came to a stop. Only Prahlada who neither heard nor saw him, sang on, and Hiranyakashipu stood aghast, realizing he had been disregarded. When the song was over Prahlada opened his eyes.

'Do you not know that that name is banned in our kingdom? Who taught it here?' demanded Hiranyakashipu. Prahlada stepped forward, fearless and smiling.

'I did, father,' he replied. Hiranyakashipu had not expected such a forthright, simple answer. He had been prepared for denials, accusations, counter-accusations, arguments and more denials. The simplicity and smiling courage of the boy took him by surprise and he felt cheated.

'Do you realize that you are going against the law of the country; that if it were not for your ignorance, I could have had you arrested and thrown into prison?'

Prahlada answered very respectfully: 'But, my king and father, I do not do this out of ignorance. I know what I am doing; I am fully aware—'

'You, you talk of awareness,' broke in the king, covering his discomfiture with a laugh. 'You, a child, with the down on your cheek scarcely grown. What do you know of these things?' Turning, he looked at Shukra. 'I now see that you were the wrong choice for a teacher,' he said coldly. 'The boy is much too intelligent and spirited for a feeble-minded creature like you. I shall educate him myself!' Shukra bowed his head. Tears began again to run down the white stubble on his cheeks.

'Come with me!' Hiranyakashipu commanded his son, and the boy touched Shukra's feet, said goodbye to his friends and went with his father.

In the palace Hiranyakashipu spoke gently to his son. He spoke to him of the heritage of the asura people, their history, their great

66

traditions. He stressed the part Prahlada must play in that history. Softly he spoke of the affection he bore him, and about the high hopes he had of him. He reminded Prahlada of Hiranyaksha, his uncle who had been done to death by Vishnu.

'Vishnu is a betrayer of promises, a false god.' Hiranyakashipu repeated. But Prahlada shook his head.

'That is a mistake, father,' he answered. 'Vishnu alone is true, and I must do what I think and believe is right.' He did not falter as he spoke. Hiranyakashipu rose from his seat, and his presence seemed to fill that mighty palace hall.

'You are defying me,' said the king in a loud and terrible voice, 'and for that I can imprison you and even kill you! In this kingdom the only god is Hiranyakashipu, and everyone must worship only him.'

'I do not defy you, sir,' Prahlada answered gently, 'but no man should be forced to worship against his will. I cannot worship Hiranyakashipu, and still be true to myself.'

His eyes and face were alight with courage. Hiranyakashipu looked at the boy's eager, handsome face and felt his heart melt with yearning for him: 'My son, why will you not listen to me?' he wept, a piteous figure in his silken robes and glinting jewels.

Hiranyakashipu tried many ways of converting the prince. Just as Shukra had done, he too tried persuasion and appeal at first; then promise of reward and finally threat of punishment. But Prahlada stood steadfast as a rock.

'I will teach you what it means to disobey me!' cried the frustrated king, and in his anger he ordered that the rebel prince be thrown in the path of a wild elephant. The soldiers led the boy away. But their hearts went out to him: 'Give up this foolishness, Prahlada,' they begged him. 'What will it bring you but death? If you do as your father says, you will live to rule a mighty empire and you will have all you want!'

'There is nothing I want but Vishnu,' the boy answered them, smiling. They marvelled at his courage and single-mindedness, and wept as they laid him in the path of the wild elephant.

Crowds of people came to see the terrible spectacle, some out of curiosity, some to cheer, but most, like the soldiers, to weep. As they watched, they saw the boy's lips moving, and heard everywhere in the air, whispering echoes of his voice taking Vishnu's name.

'Why, even the fear of death does not stop him!' cried the astonished people. But Prahlada was not to die. The wild elephant that rushed out, madly trumpeting, raising great clouds of dust, stopped short when it came before him, and stood there, as if listening. Miraculously subdued, flapping its great ears and whisking its tail, it knelt upon its forelegs before the boy, and lifted up its trunk for him to climb upon. The people saw Prahlada rise and seat himself on the elephant.

Enraged more than ever, Hiranyakashipu ordered Prahlada to be thrown down a high cliff to what would be his certain death. But once again there was a miracle, and as the boy, singing the holy

name, fell through the air, Vishnu's arms caught him and held him, and he came to no harm. He returned to the palace singing Vishnu's song still—and all the people sang it with him.

'Is it possible?' muttered Hiranyakashipu. And now a madness had begun to take hold of him.

'Burn him alive!' he cried, and he would not heed the tearful pleas around him—neither of his wife and queen, Prahlada's mother, nor of his subjects, the vast numbers of people he ruled over. But the flames did not touch Prahlada. As he entered the fire, the burning flames turned to fresh flowers, and cool breezes blew all around him, murmuring his song of Vishnu's love.

Prahlada was starved in torture chambers and flogged with leather

68

straps—but his spirit could not be broken. Vishnu was always with him, protecting him.

'Still alive?' exclaimed Hiranyakashipu in a frenzy when they brought him in chains before his throne. 'And still defiant?'

'I do not defy you, father,' Prahlada said again, 'and if I am alive it is all Vishnu's doing!'

'That name,' screamed Hiranyakashipu, 'It is torture to my heart. I tell you, Vishnu is false!'

'Only Vishnu is true, father,' Prahlada replied. 'All else is false.'

'You lie!' shouted Hiranyakashipu. He rose from his throne and with his mace in his hand, came down the marble steps to face the prince.

'You have never seen Vishnu, you fool. Have you, have you?'

'Why yes, father, I have seen Vishnu,' smiled Prahlada. 'Wherever I look, I see him . . . .' Hiranyakashipu stared into the smiling face and the clear eyes. Was the boy mad? Or . . . or . . . . He shuddered at the thought that followed.

'You *see* him?'

'Everywhere and all the time!' Prahlada declared joyously.

The golden rays of the evening sun crowned the boy where he stood and touched him with their glow. Hiranyakashipu's heart went out to him with all the love of a father. But he hardened himself: 'Once and for all your foolishness must be cured!' said he, grinding his teeth. 'Once and for all this dream of yours must be shattered. Once and for all I will prove to you that there is no Vishnu, that there is only the reality of the self.' But Prahlada did not hear him.

'Look father,' he exclaimed pointing westward, 'see the loveliness of the sunset flooding the sky . . . . Surely in all that beauty you must see Vishnu! Surely you must!'

'Vishnu!' shrieked Hiranyakashipu, 'Are you mad, Prahlada? I see nothing! Where is he? Where?' The asura's eyes had grown suddenly ferocious like an animal's but Prahlada answered, unafraid. 'Why father, Vishnu is everywhere!' He came closer to the king, his father, and looked into his angry eyes as he continued: 'He is there where people work and play; he is in the laughter of children and in the tears of the unhappy. Why, father,' he smiled, 'Vishnu is even in your own self.'

Strange emotions struggled in the asura's heart. Anger and sorrow and fear and then through them all he sensed another feeling that he could not understand at all—a desperate longing to see what this boy's eyes had seen and his own had been denied. With a strong effort of will he crushed this feeling. 'False words . . .' he roared. 'I will prove them false.'

He pointed a trembling finger to his throne. 'Is Vishnu in this throne?' he cried.

'Why yes!' Prahlada's eyes shone with conviction.

'And here?' Hiranyakashipu pointed to a dish of fruit.

'Indeed he is there, too,' smiled Prahlada. 'He is in the fruit's sweetness and beauty and its richness.'

'I cannot see him, I cannot see him,' Hiranyakashipu began to scream, 'and therefore I say you lie!' He was mad with rage and did not hear Prahlada's sad answer.

'If you will let love open the doors of your heart then, my father, you too would see . . . .'

'Where is he? Where?' yelled Hiranyakashipu and he began to run through the gilded palace, pointing wildly to the objects around him.

'Is he in this? And this?'

Each time he asked, Prahlada answered unhesitatingly: 'He is, father! Vishnu is everywhere! There is no place where he is not.'

Suddenly Hiranyakashipu halted. With slow, deliberate steps he began to approach the boy. His eyes were fierce and intense. His thoughts seemed to have come together now to one focal point. As he drew nearer and nearer the boy he looked like a wild animal stalking its prey, and his voice came out in a deadly hiss: 'If I prove that you lie, then that will be your death, Prahlada. If I prove your words false, I will tear you to pieces!'

He now towered over Prahlada like a mountain. But Prahlada did not flinch. Hiranyakashipu stared at him for a while, then began to move backwards. He moved towards the mighty central pillar that held up the colossal palace. As he did so, the sun went down. 'Tell me,' said he, his voice menacing, his words slow and deliberate, 'is Vishnu in this pillar?' And he added: 'Be careful of what you say, Prahlada, be very careful; for you will have to answer with your life.'

Prahlada's ringing voice went echoing through the palace: 'Father, Vishnu is in that pillar.'

There was a moment of stunned silence. Then in a terrible voice Hiranyakashipu cried: 'Vishnu, if he speaks the truth, then reveal yourself, and I shall fight you and make short work of you!' He raised his mace and brought it down upon the pillar.

There was a flash of blinding light and a deafening crash. The universe went whirling and demon-winds screamed, as the mighty pillar shuddered and shattered. A strange being sprang out of the crashing ruins of stone and brick and rubble. Through great, swirling clouds of dust the apparition leaped. He was neither human nor animal and yet he was both, for his head and shoulders were those of a maned lion, while the lower half of his body was that of a man.

'Why,' gasped the king, staggering back, 'what . . . what does this mean? What plot is this? And who . . . who . . . who are you?'

The people stared terror-stricken, and saw Hiranyakashipu, the giant, seem suddenly shrunken and dwarfed by the being before him. And they saw how Prahlada had gone down on his knees and how the chains that had shackled him had miraculously slipped away and fallen to the ground. And then they heard a roar: 'Hiranyakashipu, you had begged that neither man nor beast should bring about your death. Do you remember? Well! . . . Look at me! Look carefully at me, Hiranyakashipu! I am Narasimha. I am not an animal. Only part of me is animal. Look again, Hiranyakashipu! I am not human! For only half of me is man. And so shall your end come—from one who is neither animal nor human.'

Narasimha approached the king, who stood staring before him, rooted to the spot, and unable to move.

'See, Hiranyakashipu,' he went on, 'the sun has set in the western sky. Day is dead; but the moon has not arisen, and so the night is not yet born.' The yellow lion-eyes pierced into Hiranyakashipu's. 'Do you remember, asura, I had promised that death would touch you neither in daytime nor at night! And do you see now why I choose this twilight hour to bring you to your end?'

With an enormous bound, the man-lion sprang at Hiranyakashipu and lifted him up as he would have done a child. He strode with him to the threshold that separated the world inside the palace from the world outside. He sat there on his haunches and took Hiranyakashipu upon his mighty knees.

'This shall be the spot of your death,' he said, 'neither inside the house nor outside—it is just as you had wanted, is it not?'

But Hiranyakashipu, lying in Narasimha's arms, was looking intently into the man-lion's face. He seemed not to hear the arguments Narasimha offered. A peace was stealing into the asura's eyes, casting out the angers and struggles of many days.

Narasimha went on: 'No weapon shall kill you, Hiranyakashipu—neither arrow, nor spear nor mace nor sword. For you, death will come from the claws of a lion.'

'Lion?' whispered Hiranyakashipu suddenly, and his eyes lit up with the smile that broke upon his lips.

'What lion? Vishnu, do you think I am deceived because you have changed your name and form? Do you think I cannot see that you are no lion, but Vishnu, come for my life?' And he chuckled softly, as if to himself.

'Prahlada was right,' he said, and his voice was faint now. 'And all along I knew too . . . only I had to find out.'

Narasimha's claws began to tear out his vitals, but the asura continued to speak, with painful, tortured breaths. 'I knew,' he gasped, 'I knew all the time. Only I had to find out for myself. And now I am at peace. For, in the hour of my death, god holds me in his arms.' Those were his last words. For he smiled after that as a vast happiness flooded his heart and his turbulent life came, at last, to an end.

There was blood everywhere that night. It flowed over the palace floors and over the stones of the terror-stricken city. Crowds surged around the palace, as the news of Hiranyakashipu's death spread. They stopped short at the great front door where his mangled, blood-drenched body lay on the floor with Narasimha sitting across it. At the sight of it they stood petrified and silent . . . for they

who had grown up in his shadow could not believe that he was dead. Fear clutched at their hearts, and the silence of fear was around them.

It was in that silence that Prahlada began once more to sing. He sang again the song of Vishnu and this time there was grief in the melody and tears were running down his face for his father who was dead. Somehow the grief made the song sound sweeter in the people's ears. They remembered Hiranyakashipu again, and this time they remembered the rugged dignity about him, his savage greatness, and their own tears flowed. And through their tears they saw Narasimha rise with the asura's immortal soul in his hands. They gazed at Narasimha's face and saw how the anger and ferocity had gone from it at the sound of Prahlada's song of love. They recognized in it the face of Vishnu, the merciful, and they knew that he had come among them at last according to his promise, to destroy evil and restore good.

74

4

The Marriage of Shiva

In the beginning of time, when Brahma had newly created the universe, he named Daksha Prajapati, or chief, of the gods. He nominated Daksha the keeper of custom and tradition, the upholder of law and authority. When Daksha married Prasuti, daughter of Manu the law-giver, Brahma himself performed the ceremony and blessed it.

Daksha took his position very seriously. Not for him the pranks and idle play of the lesser gods. He was very conscious of his importance and insisted that everyone around him acknowledged it too. He moved into a grand and impressive mansion, and took, for his sons-in-law, the shining gods in the heavens and made them subject to himself. Fifty-nine of the gods were married to fifty-nine of Daksha's sixty daughters, and Daksha celebrated the marriages in grand style. The sons-in-law considered themselves very fortunate to be accepted by Daksha. To be married to his daughters was an important mark of rank.

Whenever Daksha performed his religious ceremonies and rituals, all the gods who could get an invitation would flock to them—for it was thought a great honour to be invited. The gods would come in their gilded chariots, riding through the clouds and the rainbows, and troop into the great hall of sacrifice with their wives and children and their retinues of servants.

The women—Daksha's daughters—seemed to live for these great days. There was all the excitement and flurry of preparation—the choosing of clothes and jewellery to wear, the discussion about who would or would not come. Above all, there was the thrill of going home to their parents. They were inordinately proud of their father, Daksha, who was held in such great respect and awe.

And so, Daksha's glittering world was firmly established. Nothing was allowed to disturb its even tenor. Everything was done in this world according to ancient custom and tradition, and Daksha ruled it with a stern hand. He performed mighty sacrifices and ceremonies

in endless succession, and people, flocking to them from everywhere, were impressed by their splendour. Daksha's influence increased even more and men and gods vied with each other to be recognized by the old man. So important did Daksha grow, that the heavenly beings began to bow down and worship him.

It was no wonder, therefore, that Daksha was well satisfied with things as they were and did not want any change. There came a time when Daksha began to believe that his world was the centre of all creation, the centre of time itself; that it would continue without end and without change, for ever and ever. There was no stir of any kind in that world; no questions were asked, no doubts expressed, no challenge offered. Everything was well-ordered and smooth-sailing.

Daksha surveyed his dominion with a proud eye and was pleased with what he saw.

Nothing can, however, be really perfect, and there was one thing in Daksha's life that caused him intense annoyance: that was the strange, and, as he saw it, totally foolish behaviour of his youngest daughter, Sati. At the thought of her, Daksha frowned darkly. Sati

was not like her other sisters—had never been. Their incessant talk of clothes and jewellery did not interest her at all. She enjoyed her father's ritual sacrifices but all the pomp and show and glitter of which Daksha and his family were so proud, left Sati unimpressed. Her eyes gazed out beyond it all into the distant, blue mountains. She would wander from the palace into the countryside, gathering flowers and berries, playing with the creatures of the wild, or talking and laughing with the humble peasants. Nothing and no one could keep her indoors. Nothing could rouse her interest in the things her father and family considered so important—the rank and status of people, the opinion of others, tradition, custom and orthodoxy.

In Daksha's world there was no greater crime than to be different, and the Prajapati and his fifty-nine daughters viewed Sati's independent ways of thought and behaviour with unease and displeasure. They could not understand her; but neither could they put their finger on what it was that upset them: for Sati, for all her independence, did no wrong and hurt no creature. There was a goodness within her that came, not from adherence to rules and regulations, but from simply being herself. While her sisters took great care to live by the rules laid down by their father and by

society, Sati, it seemed, adhered to some law inside herself. They simply could not understand it—and because they could not understand it, they could not forgive it either.

And then, one day, it came to their knowledge that this girl had actually said she was in love with Shiva, the god of eternity! The news was whispered from ear to ear in Daksha's land. Heads shook, eyebrows lifted, mouths fell open as the rumour spread.

'Sati in love with Shiva, the naked ascetic, the wandering madman of the snowy heights! What is the world coming to?' people exclaimed, their eyes shining at the prospect of all the gossip and excitement that this rumour promised.

But Daksha was furious when he heard it. He hated Shiva. In his eyes Shiva was an outcast, a blot on society and a disgrace to all respectable folk. Shiva called himself a god and yet he went about dressed like a beggar—a tiger skin and a snake for garments, skulls strung together for ornaments, and ash from the cremation ground smeared all over his body in place of the fragrant sandal-paste that good, decent people used. Daksha did not approve of Shiva's strange dress nor of his vagrant ways. And yet he might have forgiven him everything had Shiva given respect where respect was due—namely to himself. The Prajapati expected all to recognize and honour him, but Shiva, who lived on Kailasa seemed not even to be aware of Daksha or Daksha's world. Shiva was the only god who had passed by Daksha without bowing before him on that day when Brahma had made the old man Prajapati. It was not that Shiva had been deliberately disrespectful. It was simply that he had been absent-minded. His thoughts had been on other things, which he obviously considered more important and of far more consequence than Daksha, the Prajapati.

Nevertheless, Shiva's behaviour stung Daksha who was not used to being ignored. He got up in anger and abused Shiva with bitter and scornful words, ridiculing his poverty, his ragged appearance and his wandering ways. What increased Daksha's fury a thousandfold was the realization that even this anger and venom had not touched the god of Kailasa at all. Shiva scarcely heard him—his mind seemed to be on bigger things. Daksha gnashed his teeth in anger. He swore he would have nothing to do with Shiva. Shiva had become his chief enemy. And now Sati, his child, declared herself in love with the man he hated so bitterly.

'She is a disobedient, wicked and rebellious girl!' Daksha exploded when Prasuti fearfully broke the news to him. 'And you have spoilt her!'

'She is still only a child,' Prasuti ventured.

Daksha glared at her, nostrils flaring.

'She defies me! That wisp of a girl dares to defy me, Prajapati of the gods!'

Daksha had Sati brought before him. He questioned her and she hid nothing from him. Standing before him in all her youthful loveliness, Sati's answers were clear and true. There was no mistake; she loved Shiva, the god of eternity, with all her being, had loved him all along and would always love him.

'Foolish, wicked girl!' Daksha thundered. 'Do you not know that he is the foremost of my enemies, that I hate him with every pore of my body . . . .'

'That is only because you don't really know him, father,' Sati protested. 'You only see the unimportant things about him—his outward poverty, his ragged appearance. You have never seen his goodness, his shining intelligence, his wisdom, his infinite understanding . . . .'

'Why, she is madder than I thought,' spluttered Daksha, purple in the face, 'and she has the nerve to answer me back!'

His eyes blazed, his voice grew menacing: 'Stupid child! Do you think you will escape punishment for this behaviour?'

'But I love him, father,' cried Sati, her eyes filled with tears; 'I love Shiva, can't you understand?'

Daksha could not. 'A wandering beggar, ragged and disreputable!' he stormed, pacing the room in his anger. 'What has he to his name? Nothing! No home, no family, no position, no property, no learning! Are you not ashamed of declaring yourself in love with him?'

'Oh, father!' Sati's voice was full of compassion. 'Why will you not see beyond these things into his great and good heart? Why do your eyes not see the radiance of his face?'

Her own face glowed with warm passion as she continued: 'You say he has no home. But do you not see, father, that his home is everywhere, precisely because it is nowhere? You say he has no family. Do you not see that because Shiva is alone, all the world is his family . . . .'

'You shall not mention that name in this palace!' Daksha shouted her down. 'It is a shame and a disgrace!' And he ordered the girl to be confined to her room until she came to her senses. He was in a towering rage. 'We must get her married off at once,' he roared. He clapped his hands and his attendants came running. 'Make preparations for a swayamvara,' he commanded them. 'Invite a gathering at which Sati, my daughter, shall choose her own husband. Send out invitations to all the gods . . . .'

The attendants began to bustle about when he shouted to them to stop. 'Did I say all the gods? Well, that was wrong—there is one who calls himself a god whom you may not invite: Shiva! No invitation is to go to Shiva!'

Later, Daksha had Sati brought before him. He told her about the swayamvara he was arranging for her so that she might choose a worthy husband. Sati blushed. With her head bent she thanked her

father, and her heart filled with hope and joy; she did not for an instant doubt that Shiva whom she worshipped day and night, whom she considered greater than all the gods, would be among the guests at the swayamvara. Only Prasuti, listening to her husband's words and seeing her daughter's hope-filled eyes, felt uneasy. Prasuti remembered how the first word Sati had lisped when she was a baby was Shiva's name; she knew how Sati loved the god of Kailasa with her whole being. Prasuti reminded Daksha very gently about these things, but he waved her impatiently away. He believed he had everything in hand.

The swayamvara was magnificent. Handsome and richly attired, the gods glittered as they stood before Daksha, waiting upon his every word. They bowed to him and he swelled with pride. The next minute, however, his face twisted, as a memory, dark and bitter, arose in his mind. Why did the thought of the hated, the despised Shiva return to him again and again, tormenting and torturing him in his secret heart? Why could he not dismiss Shiva from his mind . . . Shiva, who had never bowed to him, had never been impressed by his wealth, learning or position?

'Well, he will not be at today's swayamvara,' he muttered

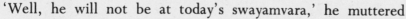

savagely, 'and the foolish girl will be forced into a sensible choice.'

Dressed in her bridal attire, Sati entered the courtyard where her suitors sat waiting. She looked very beautiful as she stood in the centre. Now she must make her choice. At a word from her father, she lifted her eyes. Her glance rested briefly upon each expectant face. Slowly she walked round, once, twice, three times, and then she returned to where her father stood, lip trembling, eye perplexed. The guests shifted uneasily in their seats, and Prasuti caught her breath. Daksha was smiling, a small, secret smile of triumph. 'Choose!' he whispered to his daughter. 'They are all here—choose the one you want for your husband.'

But Sati shook her head. Her face paled as suddenly it had come to her that her father, mighty Daksha, Prajapati of the gods, had cheated her. He had deliberately left out the one god she had set her heart upon. She felt the ground tilt beneath her feet, the heavens circle madly round her. 'You must choose!' Daksha whispered angrily. 'To go back now would be a shame and a disgrace!'

'No!' she cried out in her anguished heart, staring at the gaudy splendour around her. 'Never, never, never!' All her being went out to Shiva, the god of the mountains. 'Oh, my beloved Shiva!' she whispered, eyes closed in prayer. 'If I have loved you truly, with all my heart, then take my garland and receive me.' And she threw the garland into the empty air.

In an instant, the guests, wonderstruck, saw Shiva himself, the mighty god of eternity, standing before them all. Sati opened her eyes wide with rapture to find that the garland she had flung in despair, was around his neck. Daksha might fume and storm and rave and tear his hair, but he must now give her away to the despised Shiva. He did so, but with very bad grace; and when she touched his feet in farewell, he turned coldly away from her and would not give her his blessing.

But Sati felt neither hurt nor anger. In her heart was a singing happiness that left no place for such feelings. She was married now to her Shiva and was going with him to live among the snow-clad mountains.

The gods sped past them in their chariots.

'I have no chariot,' said Shiva. 'There is only the patient bull Nandi, my faithful servant. He will guide us while we travel slowly up the rugged mountain paths.'

'Does it matter?' asked Sati. 'I shall be with you and we will go together; we will talk together, be silent together, do all things together hereafter. What more can I wish for than that?'

So Sati entered her new home all made of drifting snow and icy vapours. All around stood the white mountains, immense, silent and immeasurably beautiful. Not even in her wildest dreams had she imagined such grandeur, such majesty, such loveliness as that which now surrounded her. She saw them in their many moods: she watched the dawn touch them with its soft pink flush. On clear days their brilliant whiteness dazzled her eyes, and yet she could not look away, so entranced was she by their shining glory; and when she woke at night, the mountains stood there: still, and darkly mysterious under the twinkling stars, or suffused with the radiance of the moon.

82

Their life was simple, their food homely. Her husband had no costly gifts to give her. She wore rough home-spun cloth such as the hill women around her wore, and the only ornaments she possessed were the necklaces and bracelets that she strung for herself from the flowers that grew on the lower slopes. And yet she made a home for herself and her husband, and, while he sat in meditation upon the peak of Kailasa, she spent her time adorning that home and making it beautiful with clever, loving hands. Their nearest neighbours lived a long distance away. But when they heard of her coming they flocked to see her, bringing with them their small, humble gifts—a new-born lamb or an earthen jar of wild honey, a pot of freshly drawn milk, vegetables or fruits, or a measure of grain from their fields. They brought with them their children and their young brides that she might bless them. Shiva they had worshipped, but always from a distance, with great respect, awe and fear; but Sati they loved, for she laughed and talked with them, and she walked with them to their fields and they saw, how, at her coming, the earth rejoiced, the seeds within it swelling and bursting with life.

One day there came, to their solitary home, a rare visitor from the heavenly regions, and Sati smiled with pleasure at his coming. But Shiva looked less pleased. 'Narada!' Shiva grumbled, as he watched the ochre-clad figure find his way up the rocky path. 'He's rarely up to any good! He's an idler and talks too much. He makes trouble wherever he goes.'

'Not if you know how to handle him,' answered Sati, with the wise and wordly look that she liked to put on from time to time. 'You can't deny that Narada is amusing and entertaining and that he can sing most delightfully!'

Shiva admitted reluctantly that she was right. In any case, they could not turn him away now, for he was already at the door, the light, delicate fingers of his left hand plucking rhythmically at the strings of his veena, his right hand clicking a pair of cymbals. He smiled, and his smile lighted up his dancing eyes—such eyes they were—that seemed to laugh and sparkle and brood and dream and grow merry and grow sad all in an instant. You could never tell what Narada was thinking.

'Nothing worthwhile, you may be sure,' muttered Shiva. 'He's a mischief-maker and a gossip. You be careful, my beloved,' he said to Sati in an aside, 'and take his talk and his chatter with a pinch of salt.'

Sati smiled and nodded as she welcomed the visitor. Shiva did not

stay long and in a little while he left them.

'Ah!' smiled Narada, making himself comfortable. 'This is heaven indeed—a heaven where a man may find peace and tranquillity, far from the noisy crowds and the clamour of the cities. Here, in silence, amid the rustic simplicity . . . .'

On and on he chattered, never at a loss for words, while Sati bustled about bringing him food and drink. He had a hundred amusing stories to tell, and she listened eagerly; the afternoon passed as if on wings. Later, he sang and she persuaded her grave husband to come and listen. So beautifully did Narada sing that even Shiva could not help praising him. He was quite taken by the music and allowed himself to relax and enter into the mood of that charming household scene.

'Well, well,' he said to Narada. 'You certainly travel a lot, don't you? And what has been happening in the other worlds? What news of the people we know?'

Sati sat before them, preparing betel leaves. Her hands were busy, but her ears were wide open for the titbits of news that Narada always brought with him.

'Well, Prajapati Daksha's house is again stirring with activity,' began Narada and, with a sidelong glance at Sati, he continued as if correcting himself, 'Of course, you must know all about the sacrificial ceremony. I don't have to tell a daughter about the happenings at her father's house, do I?'

'Oh, but you do, you do,' Sati begged of him. 'We live so far away from everyone, out here in the mountains, that we get very little news. Do tell us, Narada, do tell us! Are my parents and sisters well? What is this new sacrifice that my father is planning to perform?'

'Well, I'm surprised you haven't heard of it,' Narada answered, 'because everyone is talking about it in the three worlds . . . .'

Here Shiva cut in a little coldly. 'We live quietly here, Narada, and I do not listen to gossip.' He was beginning to be sorry that he had encouraged Narada.

'This isn't gossip!' Sati was quick to say. Was there a hint of sharpness edging her voice? 'Surely, news about one's home isn't gossip! And, is it strange that a daughter should want to hear about her parents?'

'Well, perhaps, it isn't . . . .' Shiva conceded, but he did not sound altogether pleased. Sati turned to Narada and smiled with pleasure as she begged him to go on. And as Narada spoke, the words tumbled out of his mouth—living, quivering, flaming words of joy and beauty. His fingers began to strum the veena and the cymbals began to jingle as if with a life of their own. Soon Narada was weaving out the story of the ritual sacrifice that was to be held, in poetry and song, in language so rich, so exquisitely melodious, that Sati's hands ceased their activity and lay still upon her lap, as if they too were listening. Indeed all her being was listening, thrilling to the music and the poetry. And in her mind's eye she saw once more Daksha's great, stately mansion that had been her childhood home; she saw the preparations that were being made for the sacrificial fire, the scented firewood being stacked in the appointed place, the vessels of silver and gold holding butter, grain and milk: the burnt offerings and libations for the ceremony. His songs conjured up for her the fragrance of incense and flowers, the throb of drums and the music of pipes, the clatter of horses' hooves outside, the gay laughing voices of her sisters and the rustle of their glowing silks. Once more she saw her father, tall, stern-lipped and very dignified, respected by all the gods; in her ears rang again the deep-toned chanting of the Vedas. She sat in a trance, lips parted and breathing hard, and Narada sang on.

'All the gods and the goddesses will be there,' Narada repeated. 'They have been specially invited . . . .' And he began to name them, one after the other, her sisters, the daughters of Daksha and their husbands. Fifty-nine of them he named and then suddenly he stopped and turned red. He began now to stammer, awkward and embarrassed: 'Oh . . . of course . . . of course . . . you too must have . . . must surely have got your invitation . . . the youngest daughter . . . is the father's favourite, is she not?'

And now it was Sati's turn to blush. She turned her face away to hide her embarrassment. But Shiva, looking steadily into Narada's eye with his piercing deep eyes, said gently but very firmly, 'No, Narada. We have no invitation, nor do we expect one. It is really all for the best and we are happy where we are.'

'Of course, of course you are,' Narada interposed soothingly, hastily; and then, smiling his charming smile, went on, 'What is a sacrificial ceremony after all? Empty words, glitter, pomp, meaningless ritual . . . for myself, give me any day the loveliness of these mountains, the simple peasant people . . . .' He glanced out of the corner of his eye at Sati, but she was sitting still, her hands idle upon her lap, her eyes unseeing. And she was biting her lip to steady its trembling. A doubt crossed Narada's mind. Had he perhaps said too much? His tongue—had it slipped out of control and run away with him? 'I must learn to hold it . . .' he sighed. He meant no harm. But his tongue—it seemed to have a separate life of its own. People said he made mischief wherever he went. 'It isn't I that makes the mischief,' he thought as he picked up his veena and cymbals and made for the door. 'It really is not I! It is my tongue . . . .'

Sati sat very still after Narada had gone. Indeed, she scarcely noticed his going, and it was Shiva who saw the minstrel to the door and closed it after he had gone. Sati's mind was far away; the music and the words of Narada's song lingered in her ears.

'Come, let us play a game of chess,' Shiva cajoled her, hoping to draw her attention. He arranged the pieces on the chess cloth. But Sati's mind refused to dwell on the game, and after a while she pushed the pieces away, and went back to her musing.

'Why, what is the matter?' asked Shiva, who had forgotten Narada's visit already. Sati looked up.

'I want to go to the sacrifice,' she burst out tearfully.

'But, my dearest,' protested Shiva, 'we have not been invited . . . .'

'A daughter does not need an invitation to her father's house,' retorted Sati.

Shiva sat by her and took her chin in his hand. Very gently he turned her face towards him. 'No, she does not,' he agreed and then added deliberately: 'She does not need an invitation if she is loved and wanted there; if she has married a man her father approves of.'

His face grew very serious, though his eyes continued to look into hers with a great tenderness. 'Make no mistake, Sati,' he said. 'Your father hates me and despises me. And because you are my wife you will not be welcome in Daksha's home.'

'He hated you and despised you,' Sati answered, 'but that was a long time ago. Time has gone by since then and my father will have changed . . . .

Shiva laughed. 'Daksha change? Sati, how innocent and childlike you are! Have you not understood that Daksha cannot, will not change, that he is opposed to change; that he is the god of the established order . . . .'

'I do not understand what you are saying,' Sati interrupted him irritably.

She slept restlessly that night. 'It's lonely here,' she kept thinking discontentedly. 'There's no one at all to talk to . . . .' And in the morning she continued to be silent and remote. Shiva, interrupting his meditation from time to time, came to her and tried to coax her into a happier frame of mind. But she would not speak except to remind him of her desire to go to Daksha's sacrifice.

'Try and understand,' begged Shiva. 'Try and be sensible. You do not belong to Daksha's world. If you go back to it there is no knowing what might happen.'

But she shook her head. 'What do you know of a daughter's feelings?' She flung at him, 'And you who have no parents, how can you understand a father's heart?'

Shiva's temper rose. 'I am a husband,' he answered coldly. 'And I

mean to be obeyed as a husband. You *shall not* go! I forbid you to.'

At that Sati looked up. Her eyes shot fire. In an ominously low voice she repeated his words: 'Forbid me to go! Did you say "*forbid*"? Did you say "*shall not*" to me? To me, who am the mother of all creation? I will show you whom you oppose . . . . .'

She rose and, before his eyes, she swelled until she was bigger than all the universe. He saw the heavenly bodies revolve in her eyes, the stars sparkle in her hair. He saw the past, the present and the future merge in her tremendous mouth. He trembled and cried out in terror, but the vision passed, and then he saw her as the sweet virgin, Kanya Kumari, yearning for him to come and court her. But when he reached out to touch her, she was Kanya no more, but

Shitala, fearful goddess of smallpox, fever and plague; Shitala who haunted dark lanes and alleyways where rats scrounged among scraps and foul things for food. He shrank away at the sight, but the next moment Shitala had gone and Gauri stood before him—Gauri, the gentle earth mother who nourished the soil and made it fruitful, at whose command the fields grew green and wild flowers blossomed. Then he saw Gauri's face change, and he heard wild cries as Kali appeared before him, black-faced, red-tongued Kali, dancing her frenzied dances on the field of battle and screaming for the sacrifice of raw human flesh and warm human blood. Space spun

89

and rocked about him, and he saw her change again and become Durga on her lion, brandishing her shining weapons of war. Then Durga vanished and there appeared before his eyes, Tripurasundari, queen of the skies and the rugged mountains. So he saw her in a thousand, thousand forms and breathless with fear he cried out to her to forgive him. And when he did that, she became once more the sweet and soft-voiced Sati whom he had married and whom he loved. 'Let me go, my dearest,' she begged him. 'It is so long since I have seen my mother.' Tears welled up in her eyes and her voice was very small and Shiva could hold out no longer.

'Go then, if you must,' he sighed. Her eyes lit up at his words. But Shiva grew even more worried than before. 'I am afraid for you, my dearest . . .' he murmured, but she cut him short.

'What has to happen must happen!' she answered soberly. 'No one can stop the course of destiny.'

Shiva nodded. That was perhaps true . . . and yet . . . he wished so much that she would not go. But Sati was all bubbling eagerness and joy. She could not wait to start.

Accompanied by the faithful old Nandi she went down the mountain track. She walked as if on air. Shiva slowly turned back and returned to his place of meditation.

Daksha's hall of sacrifice was crowded with people. They sat looking solemn and important in the places that, Sati knew, were given strictly according to rank and status. She recognized her sisters and brothers-in-law. They were dressed in silken robes and adorned with priceless jewels. Their painted faces were like masks, but oh! they were beautiful masks—or so it seemed to Sati because of the love welling up in her heart. Her eyes travelled further beyond them, to the centre of the hall where the great fire burned. They lighted on her father Daksha where he sat, pouring out the libation, and she smiled tenderly. Daksha was chanting the Vedas in his deep voice, leading the chorus of thousands of priests. Around him stood the vessels of gold and silver gleaming like suns and moons and stars.

It was all very solemn and grand. Sati stood still, smiling. Only her eyes continued to search eagerly. When she saw her mother she gave a little happy cry. Flinging out her arms she entered the hall. She ran past all the grand and important people and went towards the place of sacrifice.

As she did so, there was a small movement among the guests. She saw the mask-like faces turn, the fine-drawn eyebrows lift, the eyelids flutter and open. She saw surprise spread over the faces, and then the derision in the twisted smiles that began to appear on the painted lips. She saw her sisters nudge each other. She heard them snigger. But it did not occur to her that *she* might be the object of their ridicule—she and her rough garment of yellow, home-spun cloth and the wild flowers in her hair.

She ran to the place of sacrifice where her parents sat and prostrated herself at their feet.

'O my father and my mother . . .' she whispered, her heart overflowing with love.

Daksha turned. His eyes opened wide in anger. His features contorted. She heard the swift intake of his breath: 'Do you dare—' he hissed, 'dare come here again, you shameless creature, when I

90

have cursed you and cast you from my house?'

Sati paled, but she did not flinch. 'A child's love turns a father's curse into a blessing,' she said very distinctly; and though her voice was soft and gentle it reached every listening ear, 'else how can it be that I have found the greatest happiness any woman can desire—a husband, so noble, so good, so loving as Shiva . . . .'

'Do not speak of that man in my presence,' Daksha answered, crimson with fury. The veins on his forehead swelled and throbbed with rage and he began to scream out abuse at the absent Shiva. His voice rose higher and higher. Specks of foam appeared at the corners of his mouth. Volleys of words poured out from the hidden depths of hatred within him.

'Stop,' cried Sati, 'stop, father!' Unable to bear it she put her hands to her ears. Desperately she looked about the many-pillared hall. But the eyes that met hers were hostile and hard. Even Prasuti turned away. And all the while Daksha continued to rail against Shiva, spitting out insult after vile insult.

Suddenly Sati arose: 'Father,' she cried, 'surely you say all this out of ignorance. And so I see that it is I who must atone for the great wrong that has been done to Shiva today.' As she spoke she moved towards the sacrificial fire and with the last word she flung herself into its flames.

A shudder went through the hall. The brief, hushed, stunned silence was broken by a great shout: :'Stop her—save her, hold her!' But it was too late.

Daksha stood horrified to see the flames leap up around his daughter. Prasuti screamed and began to sob wildly, 'My child, my child! What have you done, my little one?'

The ceremonies ceased and the people crowded round the sacrifice, terrified. The priests stared, trembling and speechless.

Then, even as they all looked on, Nandi came hobbling up, weeping and cursing wildly, shaking his horns and calling to all earth and heaven to bear witness. The tears streamed down his furrowed cheeks. 'Inhuman Daksha!' he cried. 'Your sin shall not go unpunished. May Shiva's sword come down on you and sever your evil head from your body . . . .'

He stood for a minute before Sati's corpse, weeping brokenly. The flames had not touched her loveliness, only taken her life from her. Now she lay as if she was sleeping.

Nandi sobbed and sobbed, crying out to her to come back. Then he turned to rush away. At the great door he stopped his headlong flight. His weeping voice rang out again: 'And if, Daksha, if by some miracle you should live after vengeance overtakes you, then live with a goat's face and head, so that all men will know you for what you are.' The echoes of his shrill, insane voice filled the hall as he fled from the accursed place and made his way to Kailasa.

His body caked with mud, Nandi arrived at last before Shiva and fell weeping at his feet. He poured out to him the story of Sati's death. Shiva heard him, but his mind could not grasp the meaning of Nandi's words. When at last he understood, a great cry burst out of the god's throat: 'No, it isn't true. It isn't true.' He repeated piteously, clinging to Nandi: 'Say it isn't true.'

He looked about him with crazed and bewildered eyes. 'It is not true!' He repeated the words again and again. All night he repeated the same words and the hours wore on slowly. Nandi had crept into a corner and was sitting huddled there, weeping and moaning softly. He knew his master must be left alone to face the great sorrow that had come to him. Like any ordinary mortal of flesh and blood, the great god of eternity must grapple with his grief alone, for no one can enter another's well of sorrow. At last the mist-shrouded morning broke and as the grey shadows crept about him, Shiva knew in his heart that Sati, his beloved, was dead. He called Nandi to come close to him. 'Tell me again, Nandi,' he whispered. 'Tell me the whole story again. Leave nothing out. I must hear it all . . . I must see it exactly as it happened from the first to the very last . . . .' And the old servant narrated the tale. Shiva listened without interrupting. When Nandi came to the bitter end, Shiva cried out: 'Again, Nandi . . . tell it again and yet again . . . tell me every detail. Leave out nothing.'

And so Nandi repeated the story, again and again and yet again. The scene came alive before his eyes and Shiva saw it happen a hundred, a thousand times.

At last the lord of Kailasa got up. His face was grim and drained of blood, white as the ash upon his body. His eyes were like burning coals. Digging his hand into his coarse, matted locks, he drew out, with his thumb and forefinger, one single hair and held it for Nandi to see. It twisted and moved in the great god's hand as if with a life of its own. Softly Shiva let it fall. As it dropped from his fingers through the air, great comets went screaming in the skies, and the mountains of the earth tottered to their foundations and gaped. Then with the sound of planets in collision, the hair of Shiva split open as it touched the earth. From within it, hissing volcanoes

92

leaped up. Their fires touched the sky and darkened the sun. The flames converged, and a being took shape out of their burning fury. He was red-faced and many-armed and the fires of wrath leaped out of every pore of his mighty body.

Trembling, Nandi fell on his knees, recognizing the newly-created god as Veerabhadra, embodiment of Shiva's mighty anger.

'Hide, Daksha, hide—your hour has come!'

Eyes rolling in terror, Nandi saw how all around the fearful Veerabhadra each volcanic flame, each little spark, was becoming a separate demon of anger, smaller than Veerabhadra and yet bearing a terrible resemblance to him in limb and feature. Hundreds and thousands of such demons poured out from the fires, yelling and shrieking, cursing and hurling abuse. They danced strange, distorted dances and sang evil songs of hatred, crying out for blood, death and vengeance. They brandished crude weapons in their hands—knives and swords, wheels and axes, rocks, stones and the branches of trees. Their numbers seemed to multiply with every second, until there were vast hordes of them. And though they had sprung out of Shiva's matted hair, that god himself now stared vacant-eyed, beyond them. He saw nothing, heard nothing: their demented dances, their blood-curdling war whoops, their leering faces—Shiva was conscious of none of these; for, once the fatal hair had been plucked and allowed to fall from him, Shiva had relapsed into his trance of sorrow. The black waters of grief had closed over his head, and all things had ceased to be for him—all things except his limitless pain.

He was still in a daze as he stepped out of his home and began to walk. His feet took the road sweet Sati had taken—the road to Daksha's hall of sacrifice. His face was drawn and grey, the fires in his eyes were dead and there was only one cry in his tortured heart: 'Sweet Sati, my beloved. I am coming. I am coming to you.'

So he strode over many leagues until he reached the plains where Daksha's world lay. Frightened, Nandi ran beside him, panting and out of breath. The army of Veerabhadra marched around him, their fierce red and yellow banners flaming in the hot afternoon.

'Vengeance!' the demons cried, 'Blood, death, destruction!'

They moved with the speed of thought and arrived at Daksha's mansion. They stormed its gates and leaped over its walls. Shiva entered and Veerabhadra came after him. Then all was blinding confusion as the demons charged; with savage war whoops they set to work, wrecking, burning, destroying. They sprang upon the frightened people and beat them with staves and rods. They took Daksha's priests by their top-knots and threw them on the ground. They kicked the gleaming vessels of gold and silver and upset the offerings. They trampled on the grain and butter and tore the ceremonial cloth to shreds. They smashed the lamps and broke the idols. They dragged out the gods and goddesses from their hiding places and forced them to their knees. They broke Yama's staff and knocked out Agni's teeth, danced on Indra's head and cut off Saraswati's nose. They put out the sun's eye and they flogged the moon.

And all the while the fiery eyes of Veerabhadra, their leader, searched for Daksha: Daksha's end was very near.

Wherever Daksha went, there Veerabhadra's eyes followed him. 'There is no escape for you, Daksha,' they seemed to say.

Daksha, panting and weeping, took shelter first behind one god and then another. But the gods were powerless before Veerabhadra's might. With a sweep of his great hand Veerabhadra thrust them aside—all thirty-three crore of them.

Then Daksha took refuge behind Prasuti where she stood. But not for long, for there too, Veerabhadra's burning eyes found him out, and Daksha saw the great shadow of that fearful being loom before

94

him. He fell on his knees and cried out for mercy. But the eyes that
stared into his, blazing with the fire of a thousand volcanoes, held
neither mercy nor compassion.

There was the dazzling arc of Veerabhadra's mighty sword as it
flashed in the air, and Daksha's head rolled away. His trunk lay
writhing, gushing blood, on the floor. The nightmarish laughter of
demons was like the cries of hyenas and jackals.

Daksha, the Prajapati, was dead.

But Shiva knew nothing, saw nothing, except Sati's body on the
pyre. He stood before it staring and staring, and all things, for him,

had ceased to be.

Only once did his mind come briefly out of that dark dungeon of
misery: that was when Prasuti came weeping before him and fell at
his feet, begging for her husband's life. Then, and only then, did
Shiva turn his eyes once and see. He recognized the noble, grey-
haired woman and there was a flicker of feeling that stirred his heart,
as he remembered that this was Sati's mother who had nursed her
and loved her, and watched over her while she grew. His lips moved;
a ghostly whisper came from his throat: 'Let Daksha live.' And then
he was silent.

At Shiva's whispered words, Daksha's blood-soaked body began to move, and Prasuti cried out, 'He lives! He lives!' Her grateful tears fell thick and fast. But when the headless trunk rose up on its legs, when its hands began to grope blindly and search, Prasuti turned white and hid her face in her hands. Horror and anguish tore her: 'Headless!' she screamed. 'O god, is he to live that way!' And she fell on her knees again, weeping: 'Have pity, Shiva! Let him not live that way! Let him not be a monster without a head . . . a faceless thing! Death, even death would be better than that.'

But this time Shiva did not hear her. His eyes, his senses and all his being were fixed upon the lifeless form of his wife and Prasuti's sobs and entreaties could not reach him at all.

Seeing Shiva in a trance, the demons resumed their savagery. They clamoured wildly, singing their violent songs: 'Daksha must have a head!' they shrieked. 'The great Prajapati must have a face. Since Prasuti has said so, we must find him a head . . . a head . . . a head . . . a head!'

And one among them went up to a goat that was tied near the place of sacrifice. It was to have been slaughtered and offered, but had been forgotten in the terrible happenings of the day. Now it stood bleating forlornly, while all around Veerabhadra's army carried on their work of destruction. With a loud cry, the demon slashed off the creature's head and lifted it up on the point of his sword. 'Here, catch this,' he said, throwing his trophy to a companion. 'It will do for Prajapati Daksha.' The next demon catching it answered, laughing loudly, 'It will be just right for Daksha. It will make no difference, for his chanting did not sound much different from a goat's foolish bleating!'

Fresh roars of mocking laughter greeted the demon's words. They tossed the goat's head from one to another until finally they brought it to where Prasuti stood with the live writhing trunk of her luckless husband near her. The leader of the group slapped it onto the neck, and Daksha's spirit blinked at the world out of the goat's eyes and Daksha's words came out of his throat in the goat's reedy, quavering voice. The demons screamed with laughter and swore. They tormented Daksha with their coarse jests and pelted him with stones. And his goat's head jerked about in fear and his goat's voice bleated out pitifully. But Prasuti stood between him and his tormentors. She took his hand and the two slipped away from the hall, their once proud heads bowed, their spirits humbled.

But Shiva neither saw nor heard. He stood before Sati's body and his eyes would not leave her face. They seemed to be crying out to

her, entreating her, willing her to return to life. But she lay still, beyond the reach of his sorrow and yearning. And Shiva, looking at her, did not know that Daksha's mansion and hall of sacrifice lay in ruins about him, that what had been, a while ago, a place alive with hymn and prayer and with the flashing and gleaming of fine and costly things was now a hall of death, reeking of blood, echoing with the groans of the dying and the wounded. He did not see the smashed vessels, the torn hangings, and the broken idols lying strewn everywhere. He could not smell the smoke that arose from the burning things; he did not know that the gods had been humbled and shamed, that they cowered now behind the pillars, holding their breath in fear. None of these things touched him, as he stood by Sati's body, his great heart aching, his eyes burning with unshed tears.

How long did he stand thus? A century? Thousands of centuries? That too he did not know. Inside him there was only the endless ocean of grief.

But at last he moved. The people around him saw him pick up the corpse and put it across his shoulders. They saw him turn and walk through the wreckage and destruction and cross the threshold. He walked out into the world. Timidly they followed him, but his great strides covered such vast distances that they could not keep pace with him. He left them far behind and walked on.

Over the earth's spaces Shiva walked with dead Sati on his shoulder. Heavy was the burden he carried, but heavier still was the sorrow in his heart. All nature shuddered as he passed. From his burning eyes flames sprang out from time to time and at the touch of his blistering feet the rivers and streams dried up. Indra's rain vanished in fear in mid-air. Corn withered; plants died; animals and babies sickened and wasted away. But Shiva felt nothing. His whole being was steeped in the bitter sorrow of Sati's death.

'What shall we do?' wailed the mortal creatures, and in the heavens the gods echoed their cry. 'Soon all the universe will be consumed in the burning fire of Shiva's grief, and all creation will be reduced to nothingness.'

They turned in their distress to Vishnu, Narayana, beseeching him to help them. Vishnu heard their cries and descended from the skies. He followed Shiva on that bitter road that was the road to self-destruction. And, as he walked, the lord of the universe, he who preserves all things, he who sustains all life, shot arrows at the body of Sati, where it hung down Shiva's back. They struck the body, and with each arrow, a fragment of it fell to the earth. And the stricken people who lived around—the ragged, the miserable and the hungry—saw it shining on the parched ground like a star, and held their breaths in awe. Unlearned and ignorant though they were, unable to see the cause of their sorrows, yet they knew that here was something holy, filled perhaps with life-giving power. So wherever a piece of Sati's flesh fell, they put up a shrine to the mother goddess and prayed and sang to her.

At last the fifty-two arrows in Vishnu's quiver were spent; the last piece of Sati's body had fallen away and Vishnu turned back and returned to his home.

Shiva awoke as from a dream. The oppression crushing him was gone. A great burden had been lifted from him and its fearful heaviness was no more. But there was a vast weariness in his body and the memory of the hideous nightmares that he had waded through, lingered still in his heart. Where had he been? Where was he now? Who had removed the burden from him? He remembered that he had been walking, walking . . . endlessly walking. And looking down at his feet, he saw how they had become masses of bleeding flesh. But they had brought him home at last; home to his beloved Kailasa, home from Daksha's accursed city. He lifted his dazed eyes and saw the house not far away, nestling in a little hollow of a hill, where he would rest. But as he staggered across its threshold, he knew that there was no rest here. For the memory of Sati came flooding back and his tears began to fall. The emptiness and the silence of the cottage hit him wherever he turned. The familiar, well-loved things—her pots . . . the chess game with its pieces . . . the spinning wheel, the wooden loom . . . a crumpled, dried-out flower that lay on the floor—all cried out to him in Sati's voice, mocked him with memories of her laughter and gaiety and goodness.

'Sati,' he cried out, 'Sati, why have you left me and gone?' And the echoes of his voice multiplied and the hills cried out, '. . . and gone . . . and gone . . . and gone!'

Unable to bear it anymore, he ran out of the cottage and wandered in the wilderness, crying out her name and searching for her everywhere.

He uttered her name with every breath, day and night. He whispered it to himself in his loneliness and the winds carried the sweet sound of it on their wings. He repeated it as he sat by the edge of the waters, and the brooks and streams took it up as they flowed.

The clouds and mists breathed it endlessly, and the snow-bound silence held it in its depths.

It seeped through Shiva's being. It became his one and only prayer, his endless meditation, as he sat on the peak of Kailasa.

Centuries and aeons went by. Around and about him the stars and planets came to a stop and stood still. Time ceased. Thought ceased. All things ceased. His entire being was steeped in the eternity of Sati.

5

In Worship of Shiva

In the distance, beyond the mountains and beyond the plains, deep under the rolling ocean, the gods saw another figure seated, like Shiva, in meditation. Peering closer they recognized the figure: it was a demon, the asura Taraka. Water creatures floated about his rigid body, and the seeds of plants had taken root in his hair, for he had sat thus for many thousand years. The gods began to quake and tremble: asuras in meditation meant trouble, sooner or later, for them. True, they were rich and strong, but their wealth and strength were nothing against asuras who meditated and prayed!

And then they saw Brahma flash through heaven on his great white swan and descend to the underworld. They knew he was going in obedience to the asura's prayer. Clinging to each other in terror, the gods wondered what boon Taraka would demand from him. They did not have to wonder for long, for the very next instant Taraka's voice came shattering earth and sky. They heard him demanding from Brahma that death should not come to him except at the hands of a son of Shiva. They heard Brahma grant the monster the blessing. And then they heard the sound of Taraka's hideous, triumphant, laughter:

'Foolish, foolish Brahma!' Taraka roared. 'You do not realize that you have, by giving me this gift, made me immortal. You forget that Shiva sits in meditation and is lost to the world. His heart and all his thoughts are on Sati. But Sati will never return, for she died at Daksha's sacrifice, and her body has been cut by Vishnu's arrows into fifty-two pieces that will never be joined again. How then will a son be born to Shiva? Foolish Brahma . . . your gods are doomed now and their power and supremacy are at an end.'

The gods saw the mighty asura rise from his place of meditation and fill all the seven worlds with his presence. They saw demons and men, animals, birds and all living creatures subdued as he rode over them and conquered them. They saw him turn his fiery chariot heavenward, and advance with his great demon armies behind him, and in panic the gods gathered their own hosts to meet him at heaven's gates. But Taraka was more powerful than they, and he drove them back, scattering them as leaves in a storm. Then he rode in triumph and pride into their glittering country. Once there, he kicked open the golden doors of Indra's kingdom and entered it. He seized Indra's wealth, laughing with horrible joy to see Indra's prized possession, the white horse Uchchaishravas, that had risen from the ocean of milk when it was churned. He caught Uchchaishravas by the mane and the horse's loud and frightened neighs rent the sky. Then he charged through the length and breadth of heaven and stormed Kubera's treasure houses. Kubera fled in fear, while the asura looted his palace and carried off his thousand sea-horses from their stables. At one point brave Vayu the wind-god stood before him to fight back, but Taraka seized him by his waving hair and put him in chains and cast him into prison. After that the winds and the tempests bowed down to the demon and obeyed his will.

On and on he went, from victory to victory. He shot arrows at the sun god and took from him his radiance; the moon stopped in fear at sight of him and stood still, a petrified ball of gold. Taraka swelled with pride and ambition to see the gods cowed and humbled. There came, at last, the evil hour when he even invaded the homes of the wise and gentle sages. Heedless of their protests, he carried away Kamadhenu, their cow, who granted all desires. The holy men came running out of their ashrams to see the wicked asura sailing off like a dark meteor, holding the cow by her tail.

'Beware, Taraka!' they cried. 'Beware! You have overreached yourself. Your sins will not go unpunished. Beware, for your doom is at hand!'

'My doom! Ha!' laughed the monster, throwing a contemptuous glance at them as he soared over the universe. 'I fear no doom! Do you not know that I have tricked Brahma and wrested from him the boon of immortality? My doom will come only at the hands of Shiva's son . . .*when a son is born to Shiva!*'

His mocking laughter grew louder and filled all the universe, but the holy men were not afraid.

Taraka pointed to the figure of Shiva on the peak of Kailasa and taunted them: 'There sits your Shiva, and there he will sit in his trance forever and forever. He has turned into a statue of snow. Never will Shiva forget his Sati or look at any other woman. Shiva will never marry again. He will never become the father of a child.

So, foolish sages, you will have to wait a long, long while for my doom!'

But one day Sati was reborn in answer to Shiva's prayer, though Shiva, lost in eternity as he was, did not know it. Sati was reborn as the younger daughter of Himavat, king of the Himalayas. The baby's birth was greeted with great joy in Himavat's kingdom, but no one except the gods knew that the little girl who lay kicking and gurgling in her painted cradle was Sati the eternal earth mother. Only sometimes, the eyes of Ganga, Himavat's older daughter, stared into the baby's, as if to probe their deep mystery. Ganga seemed to have found something in those dark and limpid pools of light which all others had missed. Ganga alone seemed to know, to have guessed.

The child was named Uma. Sometimes they referred to her as Haimavati, daughter of Himavat. She grew up in the palace, bringing happiness to all who saw her. But because she was Sati, had always been and would always be Sati—even though she did not know it herself—her love and devotion to Shiva continued as ever, deep and unswerving.

'Ah, now we shall be saved,' thought the gods in their heaven. 'Sati has come back and is as devoted as ever to Shiva. Now he will wake from his trance and return her love. He will marry her and there will be a son . . . .'

They saw how, even as a child, her games and play were made up of the worship of Shiva; how in her sleeping and in her waking hours her thoughts were all on him. Her parents, unlike Daksha, were delighted, for they themselves were worshippers and devotees of Shiva. Uma's childhood flew as if on wings, its golden hours spent in gathering flowers for Shiva's worship, in bringing to his shrines offerings of milk and water, brown sugar and sweet wild honey. The girls from the surrounding villages joined Uma and Ganga in their worship and they danced before the Shiva symbol. All through the night their songs and the sound of their drums and anklet-bells filled every woodland shrine in that mountainous land.

'Ah,' said the gods, 'Uma will wake Shiva up and out of their marriage a son will be born. He will save us.' But they spoke too soon. Sitting on distant Kailasa, Shiva neither saw Uma nor heard her prayers. He was steeped in his dream of Sati.

Uma grew up. In time, her friends said goodbye to their childhood and went their different ways, accompanying the husbands their parents chose for them. Ganga too went her way and led her own life. She was a strange, mysterious girl, fiercely

102

independent and freedom-loving. Gods and men loved her and wooed her, but she never stayed long with anyone. After a while she always returned to herself to follow her own independent course.

In Himavat's palace, Uma was now the only child. Alone she carried her offerings to Shiva's shrines, walking up the lonely rugged mountain paths and goat-tracks. Sometimes she walked through the forests, loving their silence, feeling their softly breathing life. Sometimes a lonely wayfarer would join her, a beggar in ochre, or a ragged goatherd, and he would marvel at her devotion and goodness.

At home in the palace, her parents often spoke to each other about finding a suitable husband for her. But Uma herself did not seem to mind that she had grown to womanhood and was still single. It was nothing to her that her friends were all married and she was still in her father's home. And when Himavat broached the subject of marriage one day, she shook her head and answered: 'My heart belongs to Shiva, dear father, and I cannot marry any other.'

Himavat was perplexed. He knew of his daughter's devotion to the lord of Kailasa, had even encouraged it himself; but he had not anticipated this situation.

He reasoned with her: Yes, he explained, he too was a worshipper of Shiva. He too loved that ascetic god of the Himalayas. But Shiva was a *god*—did she not understand that? Shiva was immortal, unreachable. Even if it were possible to climb the mountain heights where, they said, Shiva lived, there would still be the problem of arousing him from his meditation.

'I would get him for you if I could, my child,' Himavat said very kindly, shaking his white head, 'but do you not see that Shiva is beyond the reach of ordinary mortals like us?'

He advised her to continue to worship Shiva from afar, but to choose as her husband a mortal made of flesh and blood.

But this Uma would not do. Her heart, she said, belonged entirely to Shiva. If she could not have him, well, she would not have another. So with many doubts and misgivings and many prayers that things should go well, Himavat let his daughter be.

'What has to happen will happen,' he consoled himself, 'no man can change the course of destiny.'

When the demon Taraka had gone back to his underworld, the gods raised their frightened heads and began to talk to each other in whispers. '*When* Shiva gets a son . . .' The asura's words were still echoing around them in space. They turned their eyes towards Shiva and cried out to him. But in vain; the god of Kailasa sat still and unmoving. He saw nothing, heard nothing. He was lost in Sati. Though the universe and all the worlds crashed about him he would know nothing, feel nothing.

'What shall we do?' cried the gods, wringing their hands. 'How shall we wake Shiva from his meditation?'

'To wake him is not enough,' Brahma said. 'His heart must stir with love for a woman. His meditation must be interrupted.'

'How?' cried the gods.

'I have a way,' Brahma answered. He closed his eyes, and began to dream. Dream after rosy shimmering dream he spun, and as he dreamed, the gods felt all about them soft, cool rain, and a gentle breeze that set the leaves rustling. The grasses stirred and parted to make way for a youth who appeared among them . . . a slender graceful boy dressed in flowing yellow whom they recognized as Vasanta, spirit of springtime.

At his coming the air grew loud with birdsong and the humming of honey bees. Little brooklets danced out of the earth, slipped in and out of the rocks and pebbles and went gushing through the ferns. The earth rejoiced; the trees put forth buds and blossoms.

The gods were still looking on, when there was a cloud of green wings all about them and flocks of parrots rose chattering from the branches of the trees and circled above them. There was a sound of laughter, and suddenly, out of the air, there stood before the assembled divinities, Kama, the god of love, and Rati, his wife, goddess of desire.

The three spirits stood before Brahma and all the gods, and asked them the reason for their summons. Brahma pointed with his forefinger at the lonely white peak in the distance. Following the direction in which Brahma pointed, the three spirits saw a speck. They gazed at it. Then Kama gave his rather arrogant, shallow laugh. 'It is *his* heart you wish me to pierce?' And he drew out his sugarcane bow.

Rati's eyes grew coy and her soft body heaved, languorous and warm. Her full red lips parting in a drowsy smile, she murmured: 'It's a poor sage whose downfall is near . . . little does he know . . . .' She moved close to her husband and looked up at his handsome young face.

Vasanta's eyes twinkled merrily: 'Now,' said he, 'now for some fun . . . .' But he did not finish the sentence. For, as he was talking, the clouds and mists moved away and the three saw the crescent moon gleaming in the ascetic's matted hair. At the sight they paled. Uneasily they looked at each other and at the gods.

'It is Mahadeva,' whispered Vasanta at last. His eyes darted this way and that, and his voice became a frightened whisper: 'If we arouse Mahadeva's anger we will have to pay dearly.'

And the three began to back furtively away. The gods cried out to them in appeal. 'You are our only hope,' they pleaded, and told them about Taraka. Suddenly Kama tossed his flower-crowned head.

'I am not afraid,' he laughed. 'I will aim my arrow at Shiva's heart and break the power of his meditation. I will cause him to succumb to the weakness of love!'

He turned to Vasanta. 'Lead the way,' he said. 'Prepare for my coming. Make all the woodland alive with the warbling of birds and the mating calls of animals. Fill the hearts of flowers with golden honey and pollen. Then I will shoot my love-arrow and the master of Kailasa will open his eyes!'

Kama began to laugh. He swayed where he stood. His ambition, his dreams were dizzying. 'There must be a woman before him at that precise moment,' he told them, growing serious, 'and she must be beautiful. Have you such a woman for him?'

'Yes, yes,' chorused the gods. 'We have thought of that. There is a woman. Have no fear, Kama, we will lead Uma to the glade where Shiva meditates.'

'Then away with doubt and misgivings!' Kama laughed. 'It is time to start work. Go before me, Vasanta, and prepare the earth!'

'I will,' replied Vasanta, and darted up the rocky path.

Wherever Vasanta's feet touched the earth, sweet-scented flowers sprang up and adorned the countryside. Wherever Rati walked, there arose a longing within the secret hearts of things. Last of all went Kama, carrying his bow with its string of honeybees and his quiver of flower-tipped arrows.

Uma woke early. The inmates of her father's house were still asleep. From her window she could see a few stars shining in the frosty sky. In the distance was the beautiful and moving sight of Kailasa rising above the shadows, touched softly by the rays of the early sun.

Noiselessly, on tip-toe, Uma ran out of the palace door into the open. The mountains seemed to call her. She ran swiftly through the narrow winding streets of the village and came out into the open meadow. There was snow everywhere and the trees were stark and bare. She found a hilly path and decided to take that. She scrambled

106

from rock to rock, making her agile way upwards. As she climbed higher, the way became more difficult; her breath came hard and her heart throbbed painfully against her ribs. But she did not mind. She had heard of a glade where they said a holy man sat in meditation. If she persevered, perhaps she would reach that peak and make her offerings to him. Perhaps the holy man would show her the way to Shiva. All night long she had felt a yearning in her heart for the moon-crowned god. She climbed steadily, and as she went higher on those lonely tracks, she could not say why she felt a singing happiness in her blood such as she had never experienced before. How could she know that the gods were leading her on? In the afternoon she rested for a while in a small hollow of a hill. Perhaps she dozed for a bit. Then she looked up with a strange feeling of being watched. She turned her head, and there flashed past her something that looked like green and gold lightning. Three figures . . . she could have sworn she saw them! They shimmered through the snow-covered trees, and suddenly, as she looked on, the branches were gloriously, joyfully alive with leaf and blossom. There was a humming and droning of insects around her, and, at her feet, the flowers opened in wild profusion and the air was heavy with their scent. 'Why,' she thought, dazed; 'it is springtime.' She smiled to see the eagles circling above, and the small wild marmots sitting on their tails, uttering little screaming cries. She walked on, clutching her offerings.

'How beautiful it is,' she breathed, as she skirted the borders of a green lake that reflected the mountains around her. There were wooded hillocks around the lake, thickly forested with pine and cedar and fir. She plunged into the forests and emerged at last into a glade. And there in that glade she stopped and stared with wide-eyed, breathless wonder. She could not believe it . . . and yet it was true. There was indeed a yogi who sat in meditation. Around him in that glade all was still and silent. Nothing stirred; not a ripple moved upon the water. Time had ceased to be.

She stood very still, and the realization came to her that the yogi was Mahadeva. No one had told her, and yet she knew. Her heart was full of adoration. Unmoving, she stood drinking in his mystic beauty. And then she knelt on the earth and gazed at him in worship. It was at that very instant that Kama, Rati and Vasanta, hiding behind a giant cedar, exchanged looks and smiled. As Vasanta smiled, the wheel of time began once again to move, and springtime, which had paused at the entrance to the glade, entered it. Then all nature stirred with life and beauty. And now it was Rati's turn. She cast her spell on the air and desire sprang up and stirred the hearts of all living things. The goddess smiled at Kama and made him a sign; Kama lifted his bow and drew the flower-tipped arrow from its quiver. He took careful aim. But just as he was going to let the arrow fly, he felt himself tremble, felt his mouth become dry, his hands turn to ice. Kama's eyes had seen a small line in the centre of Mahadeva's forehead. Light-hearted and light-headed as he was, he realized with a chill fear clutching his heart, what might happen if that small line stirred. It was Shiva's third eye, and if it so much as blinked, all the universe, it was said, would be reduced to ashes! Kama's thoughts ceased at this point. He stood stricken with fear.

'Go on!' Rati whispered fiercely, impatiently, in his ear. 'Why do you hesitate? Shoot your arrow . . . . Let our adventure begin . . .' and at the sound of her voice Kama recovered, and his fears vanished. He grew reckless and irresponsible. His lips parted in a smile, his eyes grew insolent.

'Now . . . now!' whispered Vasanta in the love-god's ear, and Kama's arrow sped from his bow and struck the heart of the god of eternity.

Shiva awoke. From timelessness he awoke into time; there was one fraction of a second which separated the past and the present; and in that fraction of time, Shiva's mind quivered with the half-formed thought that the girl who knelt at his feet was very lovely . . . and then he realized what had happened. There was the faintest suggestion of pain near his heart, the faintest scratch on the skin outside it and a speck of red at the scratch—And at his feet . . . a poor little twig with a wilting flower at its tip! Shiva stared at it . . . . It was an arrow . . . and he recognized it. As he did so, anger blazed in the great god's blood. He had been fooled, his meditation interrupted by two silly, irresponsible, scatter-brained youths: Kama had shot that miserable arrow at him—he had dared! Suddenly the third eye of Shiva flickered. There was a blinding flash, and Shiva vanished. Where he had been, there was only the curling, ghostly mist of the Himalayas.

Behind the trees the terrified eyes of Kama and Vasanta saw only an all-devouring brilliance. The next minute the youths crumpled where they stood. They felt their limbs cease to be, their senses dissolve; and they were no more. There was nothing left of the pair but a handful of ashes.

Uma looked about her. Where all things had, a few seconds

before, been quivering with life, there now was only the grey stillness and silence of death. The vividness of the parrots and their busy chattering had ceased. A few tattered feathers in the dust were all that was left of them. The flowers had shrivelled; the grass was brown; the trees held up skeletal arms to the sky. Above all, the mound before which she knelt was empty. Shiva had gone. Where, when, how had it happened? She could not say. There had been that streak of dazzling light, and that was all. Her eyes had barely met his, her lips had barely spoken his name when it had happened. She stood up and looked bewildered about her. As she stood there, she heard a sorrowful wailing. It seemed to come from out of the scorched earth, to echo and trail away among the empty hills.

'Kama, my husband, my beloved; Vasanta, my friend, what will become of me now . . . . What will become of me?'

Uma turned her head to see a woman lamenting, beating her breast, tearing her hair. Scalding tears were streaming down her cheeks. She was crouching on the dry, cold earth, and before her was a heap of ashes.

Uma approached her, knelt beside her: 'Why, what has happened?' she whispered. But the other continued to weep.

'Kama, my beloved, you are dead and Vasanta is no more. What will become of me now? What will become of me?'

Around the two women, ghosts arose, shadowy fearful things, and moved silently through the mountains. Uma saw them, but the other woman's eyes were blind to all things; they were fixed upon the ashes before her and she continued to beat her breast and wail: 'Kama, my beloved, Vasanta, my ally, what will become of me, now? Come back. Come back!'

Uma put out her hand to touch the unhappy soul but she could not reach her. The woman's bitter sorrow was like a stone wall between them and Uma's compassion was futile. So she left her crying amidst the desolation of the bare, naked hills, and slipped away. Within her too was a vast longing, an emptiness, for Shiva had gone from her . . . and Uma's own heart was crying out for him— not indeed like this creature's, loudly, hopelessly lamenting, but with a sorrow too deep, too painful for words or tears.

'I must find him,' Uma breathed. 'Over all the universe I will wander, till I find him. For me there will be neither rest nor sleep until I have found Shiva.' So saying, she slipped away out of that glade.

'Give them back to me . . . . Give them back!' wailed Rati in

the silence. The echoes mocked her. 'I cannot live without them. I cannot be without Kama, my husband . . . .' she cried, and the shadows danced weirdly about her. She gathered the ashes in a cloth and stumbled blindly out of the glade. She did not know where she was going or what she was doing. She did not know that all her fresh young beauty had gone from her, that the bloom on her cheeks had faded, the light in her eyes grown dull.

She walked on, weeping pitifully. Her lament filled the earth like the sound of dry and bitter wind. Crows flew up in black throngs and followed her. She wandered across the blazing sky, and over the parched brown earth, her dusty hair streaming behind her, her feet bleeding and blistered. And at sight of her, the mortals were struck with fear.

The gods looked down from heaven and their eyes followed her wherever she went. They turned to Brahma.

'What have you done?' they accused him. 'See what your clever plots and plans have all been reduced to.' Brahma looked down. He saw an earth where love was dead and springtime had become bleak and ashen. Here, on this loveless earth, the birds and animals did not mate, the bees no longer carried their life-giving pollen from one flower-cup to another. Here young people did not make love or dance or sing. Around them was only the aridness of drought and the sweep of the spreading desert. Birth had come to an end and there was only death and sorrow everywhere.

Brahma and the gods continued to watch. They saw the gaunt, spectre-like figure of Rati stumbling over the stony wastes of the earth and heard the sound of her bitter wailing.

They saw the weak, helpless mortals turn their eyes to heaven. They saw them fall upon the ground and cry out to them for mercy: 'Forgive us our sins! Have mercy on us and make our earth fruitful again!'

The gods heard the mortals and turned their eyes away in shame. They had no answer. They were themselves weak and helpless.

When the answer came, it was not from heaven. The answer came resounding through the great caverns of the underworld where Taraka lived: 'Foolish Brahma—did you think you could contrive to bring about my death? Ha—you witless gods! The dream that Brahma built has crashed; Shiva has vanished, and Kama and his ally Vasanta have been reduced to ash. The earth is a desert. Shiva's son shall be my slayer, yes—Shiva's son—*when* Shiva has a son. But how will that son be born, when love is dead and birth has ceased?'

And he roared again in fearful laughter, making the mountains shake and the gods turn pale.

When Uma left the glade, Rati's lamentations were still echoing in her ears. 'Kama, my beloved, I cannot be without you.' And she heard the answering cry inside her own sorrowful heart: 'Mahadeva, my beloved, I cannot be without you.'

'But tears will not help,' Uma whispered to herself. 'And for me who has once known Shiva's face and glory there is no turning back. There is only one way to go and that is the way that leads to Shiva.'

Very quietly, very softly, she took off her ornaments and laid them aside. She would become an ascetic—she would meditate and pray, fast and do penance until Shiva came back to her. Through the days and nights, over the years and centuries, yes, through life after life she would seek him, by means of these austerities, until she found him.

So Uma set out on her great search. Like Rati, she, too, wandered over the mountains and hills of the earth . . . . She walked barefoot over desert lands and searched by the waters of the seas. Wherever she was, her heart called out to Shiva ceaselessly and she meditated constantly upon his name. Men and women saw her as she

112

went by, a wraith-like figure in white, her long hair flowing behind her, her eyes remote, yearning and searching, ceaselessly searching. Disease was spreading among them—plague and fever and the dreaded smallpox. She walked through their scorched countryside strewn with the skulls and bones of dead things. But she seemed to hear and see nothing, for all her being yearned endlessly for Shiva. The icy waters of rivers, the sun-baked blistering rocks, all were alike to her. All were places to pray in, and search in. Food and drink, sleep and rest ceased to have meaning, and she lost count of

time. Thought and speech fell away; her lips forgot all other words except Shiva's name. So centuries passed and aeons went by.

One day, she saw before her a yogi, a yellow-robed mendicant who smiled at her and raised his hand in blessing. Uma asked him if he could show her the way to Shiva.

'Shiva?' exclaimed he, as if he could not believe his ears. 'All these austerities and hardships, all this penance and prayer for *Shiva* . . . .'

'Yes, indeed!' she nodded eagerly. 'Can you show me the way to him?'

The yogi began to chuckle as if at a joke. 'That madman? That mendicant? That homeless wanderer who dances in cremation grounds? Child, child! You are a princess, delicately nurtured, beautiful, young. Many suitors ask for your hand in marriage. Why do you not choose one of them? Surely they are worthier of you than this ash-smeared, ragged being that you call Shiva . . . .'

But she smiled gently and sadly at him: 'You do not know what you are saying, yogi,' she answered him. And then she began to speak to him about Shiva and the wonder of his beauty and strength and love. She sang of the limitlessness of Shiva, his might, his glory and his all-pervading nature and the words cascaded out of her being, unendingly. So rapt was she in her song of Shiva that she did not notice the transformation that was taking place in the yogi, until the crescent moon gleamed in his hair. And then she gasped and was silent. For suddenly it dawned on her that this was no yogi at all, but Mahadeva himself whom she had yearned after. She saw Shiva's smile, tender and extraordinarily beautiful, and she felt happiness surge through every pore of her body as his arms enfolded her. And in that moment Uma knew she was Sati reborn, Sati, the eternal mother, the life that is at the heart of all things.

Together Shiva and Uma made their way towards Kailasa. The long years of separation were over at last.

On their journey they were accosted by a creature that hobbled up to them. It was Rati. Haggard of face and worn to a shadow, dressed in rags, and weeping, begging forgiveness, Rati still cried out for her husband.

Shiva looked at his wife. 'Well, what do you say, my dearest?'

Uma's eyes were wet with tears of compassion: 'I would not deny a share of my happiness to any creature,' she said, and Shiva restored Kama and Vasanta to Rati . . . not, it is true, in their physical forms, for those were burnt to ash—but he restored their spirits and made them deathless and everlasting. And so Rati's heart, too, was at peace at last. The people on earth heard the breezes murmur again and saw the soft rain fall and the miracle of springtime happen, with the budding of new flowers and the calling of birds, one to another, and they knew Vasanta had returned at last. And when they saw the love-light in the eyes of boys and girls, and heard happy young voices whisper words of love and hope, they knew that Kama too was back in their midst, Kama with his wayward, flower-tipped love-darts and his sweet sugarcane bow. They welcomed the pair with frenzied joy, danced wild whirling dances to them in their happiness, and splashed each other with colour.

114

There was a wedding: Shiva and Uma were married and all the gods came to bless them and wish them happiness. But as the gods returned home to their heaven, they remembered Taraka. 'Taraka has still to be vanquished,' they said. 'But now, we may set our minds at rest; for surely a son will soon be born to Shiva and Uma.'

And they waited for the child of Shiva to be born. But long years passed and there were no children at all.

The gods worried, grew restless and impatient. Why had Shiva not blessed his wife with children? Meanwhile, Taraka, who had cowered a little when Shiva had married Uma, regained his confidence and grew reckless once more. He laughed at Shiva's childlessness and terrorized the gods and trampled upon heaven over and over again.

But Shiva did not deign to answer the demon's taunts. He kept his thoughts to himself. And if there was a smile in Uma's heart, her lips did not betray it.

Childless? Let the demon believe it! Let no creature know; let no creature suspect that, among the sands on the shores of the ocean, there lay one tiny, quivering, shining seed, no bigger than a speck, and that the tiny seed held the son of Shiva.

The seed sparkled and shone with a fierce red light as it lay among the sands. It gave out a fiery heat like the heat of war-weapons.

Agni, whose eye was keener and more far-seeing than anyone else's, spotted it from heaven. He frowned. Was it a second Agni he saw, far away on the shores of the sea? And then his gaze, moving towards Kailasa, caught Uma's anxious eyes and he knew.

'We cannot let him lie there unprotected,' Agni thought to himself in his secret heart. 'Each minute his radiance grows and his light will proclaim him and Taraka will see him.'

He seemed to hear Uma's voice in his ear: 'You must carry him to Ganga, my sister,' it said. 'Ganga will shelter him. She will hide him from Taraka.'

Winging his way out of heaven, Agni reached the seashore. He picked up the tiny mote of living fire that was Shiva's son. As he made his way towards the waters of the river he heard the voice of Uma whisper again: 'Call him Kartikeya!' He looked up once more. She was sitting in her home in Kailasa, her hands clasped in prayer. Her thoughts had come across space and reached him again.

Kartikeya, tinier than a grain of sand, was fostered and nurtured in the waters of the Ganga, among the fish and the water creatures. The river goddess fed him and nursed him. She hid him and sheltered him from every danger. She taught him the wisdom she had gathered through the years. She sang to him her age-old songs and rocked him to sleep when he cried. He grew handsome and proud, and Ganga gloried in his strength and beauty.

One day he grew so bright that Ganga could hide him no longer. Even her eyes were dazzled. From afar the gods saw the waters of the river shining with the light of countless suns, and they spotted him in its depths.

'Who is he?' they whispered in awe. And Agni told them at last. 'He is Shiva's son, Kartikeya.'

'Shiva's son . . . ! Shiva's son . . . !' There was rejoicing among the gods.

'Hush,' warned Agni. 'Be very wary! Taraka must not know.'

But the gods were already speeding towards Kailasa where, coming before Uma, they fell at her feet. 'Give us Kartikeya, eternal Uma, for he alone can lead us to victory against Taraka's forces,' they cried.

Across the distance Uma's great eyes met Ganga's and both knew that the time had come for their son to go from them. He was a child no longer. Their hearts ached, but they blessed him as they said goodbye.

The peacock which Kartikeya rode spread its jewelled tail and carried the tall dazzling youth to the heaven of the gods, where the immortals welcomed him.

'Lead our armies, Kartikeya,' they cried, and he tossed his splendid flaming hair and laughed. Then he gathered the heavenly hosts, riding among them like a forest fire, and he held them in readiness for the war that was to come.

Meanwhile, Taraka the demon, unaware of Kartikeya's existence, had overreached himself and thrown every caution to the winds. Once more he stormed heaven with his demon hordes. But he had attacked once too often, for this time Kartikeya was ready for him with the heavenly armies behind him.

116

Suddenly, without warning, the gates opened and the fiery youth went tearing through the demon hosts, uttering fierce war cries, the weapons in his six pairs of hands flashing. Swifter than the wind he went, cutting his way through the dead and dying demons until at last he came face to face with Taraka.

'Who are you?' gasped the demon. Kartikeya laughed aloud.

'Shiva is my father, and Ganga cradled me, and fed me at her breast. I am Kartikeya, son of Uma and Mahadeva, and since your

death can come only at the hands of a son of Shiva, prepare now for your end.' And the next minute he slashed at Taraka's head with his flashing sword. It rolled from his body and the demon lay dead.

Victory was with the gods. They rent the air with their cries of rejoicing: 'Taraka is dead—! All glory to Shiva's son, Kartikeya, who has brought about the evil one's end!' There was dancing in the streets of heaven, and noisy singing, as the gods crowded round Shiva's son.

'Stay with us,' they begged him. 'Protect us and our goods, our wealth, our wives, our lands and our cattle. Lead our armies. Smash our enemies. Do not ever go from us.'

The shining youth swaggered and looked about him. 'So,' he thought, 'this is heaven—swarga.' He gazed at the sun-reflecting domes and golden avenues. How splendid swarga was! How it bustled with noise and activity. How different from Kailasa, his father's home! Kartikeya's gaze travelled to the mountain peak where all was white mist and silence. Then it turned to Ganga, where her waters sang and murmured as they flowed. 'I see nothing but loneliness there,' Kartikeya said to himself. Then he turned round and faced the gods:

'I will stay with you and make swarga my home. I will share your life,' he said. The face of his father Shiva, and the faces of his mother Uma and Ganga rose before him for a fleeting moment, then vanished as the gods lifted him upon their shoulders and carried him in triumph to their country.

6
Manasa Seeks a Devotee

Manasa Devi was the goddess of snakes. Her home was the mysterious underworld where her brother, the mighty Vasuki, reigned. Dusky-skinned and dark-haired, she was beautiful and terrible in her ornaments of shells and beads and strange wild flowers. Men feared her, for they said that she had, at her command, powerful magic spells that could strike a man dead, or take away his reason, and even his manhood. And yet they knew that she also had magic charms and potions that could heal and soothe; that could cure snakebite and even bring the dead to life. She could be vindictive and cruel, if she chose to be, so no one dared risk her anger. She was a daughter of Shiva the god of eternity, but her mother was a snake girl. When still a baby she had been taken to her father's home in Kailasa. That was in the dark and ancient days, when snakes ruled the world and were worshipped.

But there came a time when the shining gods, their wives and attendants entered the heavenly regions. The earth folk welcomed the shining ones and worshipped them with much ceremony and rejoicing. And among the new divinities was Parvati, the golden-skinned wife of Shiva. Manasa, crouching in a neglected corner, felt a deep foreboding: with Parvati's coming the days of her glory would end. Nor was she mistaken. The earth folk hailed Parvati, and forgot Manasa and her snakes, her mystery and magic and her dark beauty. Her devotees dwindled steadily in number. It was Parvati's day and, save in a few remote villages and in an isolated city or two, people ceased to pray to Manasa. She cried out for her rightful share of worship, but Shiva was lost in the meditation of the eternal, and the others paid her no attention.

The shining ones were many and strong, and the fickle humans were dazzled by the radiance. Manasa was driven out of heaven and banished to the darkness of the underworld. There she brooded and fretted, plotted and schemed, determined to win back her rightful place. At last she decided that, if she could win over a merchant prince called Chand Saudagar, his people would follow his example and she would regain some of her lost empire. Chand Saudagar was wealthy and powerful; his influence was widespread.

Manasa began to woo him. First she appeared to him in many guises and offered him even greater wealth and power than he had, in return for his devotion and worship. Treasure-houses filled with gold; precious stones from the underworld of the snakes; rolling acres of green and fruitful land; overflowing granaries—all these Manasa promised Chand Saudagar, her eyes glittering.

'Come,' she whispered in her husky, low voice, 'why do you hesitate? Do you not want to own this beautiful world?'

But Chand Saudagar, sitting in meditation before the symbol of Shiva, scarcely heard her.

She tried another way. She entered his dreams at night and once more dangled before him the things that men desire: power over people and the love of beautiful women; hope of children and grandchildren who would carry on his name after he was dead and so make his memory immortal.

'Only worship me,' she coaxed, 'and all this will be yours.'

'Worship *you*?' exclaimed Chand Saudagar. 'Worship *you*, snake woman?' and he laughed scornfully. 'Go from here, Manasa, and understand that Chand Saudagar is a devotee of Shiva and will not be shaken from his faith. He will have nothing to do with you and your snakes.'

He turned his face away. Manasa's eyes flickered and her dark face flushed very slightly. But when she spoke again, her voice was soft and cool: 'You do not know my power, Chand Saudagar.'

'Go away,' Chand Saudagar said again. 'Have I not already told you that I will have nothing to do with you?'

Her eyes narrowed as she hissed: 'Take care—take care, Chand Saudagar! The snakes of the underworld obey my word. At my command they could make short work of you and your family and all your kinsfolk.'

Her sinuous body swayed threateningly. Chand Saudagar paid no heed to her.

'You will pay for this,' muttered Manasa Devi. 'You will know what it is to slight me! Your pride will be brought to dust, and one day you will worship me!'

'Never!' Chand Saudagar answered, smiling proudly. 'Never will I worship you, Manasa Devi!'

'Never is a long, long time, Chand Saudagar,' Manasa whispered, 'and I can wait.' And she vanished from sight.

From then on she would not let him go, or allow him peace, for she was as determined as he. The merchant's dreams at night became fearful nightmares. Snakes twisted and turned about him, opening hungry mouths as if to swallow him. They seemed to coil about him, disturbing his sleep, until he woke up in an icy sweat. He grew haggard and ill with lack of sleep. And the voice of Manasa pursued him wherever he went, asking to be worshipped.

'No,' said Chand Saudagar, 'no, no, no! I will die a thousand deaths, snake woman, but I will not worship you.'

'We will see, Chand Saudagar, we will see,' Manasa muttered darkly.

One day the merchant went out into his garden to relax—a garden where, with his own hands, he had planted many kinds of flowering bushes and creepers and trees. He sat among the rare flowers that bloomed there, and the beauty that surrounded him cheered his spirit. Some distance away he could hear happy voices. After many harrowing days, Chand Saudagar felt a gentle peace steal into his weary heart.

But not for long. In a fraction of a second, it seemed to him, a shadow fell in his path and a cold wind rose as the softly curving form of Manasa took shape before him. It seemed to be made of black smoke, and yet the form was so real that he could have touched it. Then her husky voice fell on his ear and all other sound ceased:

'Fool, fool, do you not see that I can destroy all your world and leave you a beggar? Why will you not understand that all you must do is worship me to be protected against ill fortune?'

Chand Saudagar's face grew stern; his hands clenched: 'Go, snake goddess, go from here. In vain do you ask me to worship you, for I am a worshipper of Shiva.'

She was furious; 'We will see . . . .' she cried. 'I will still get the better of you . . . .' and her eyes flashed cold fire.

That night Manasa Devi's anger fell on Chand Saudagar's garden and everything in it, down to the smallest blade of grass, withered away.

When Chand Saudagar visited the garden the next morning, he saw a great rolling desolation. Where once flowers had bloomed and birds had sung, was now an empty desert. He groaned and, for a second, thought the world was going dark. Then he gasped in angry surprise as he saw Manasa Devi standing before him. She had taken

form out of nothingness. A mocking smile played about her mouth and she caressed the snakes twining about her body.

'You!' uttered Chand Saudagar. 'So it's you again.'

'Who else?' she laughed.

Her laughter was soft and low, like dripping honey. A snake coiled itself about her neck and kissed her dusky face. Her swaying form drew near to the merchant. Her steel-cold eyes probed his and she began to whisper: 'Do not imagine that what has happened has happened by chance. Understand that I am the power behind this destruction.'

She threw back her head and laughed, then brought her face close to his. 'What you have seen now is nothing to what I can do! Listen Chand Saudagar, if you bow down and worship me I will restore all this to you.' And she spread out her hands to indicate the desolate garden. Chand Saudagar steadied his senses and recovered his composure with a small effort. 'I have told you to do your worst, Manasa!' he answered angrily. 'Do you think I am afraid of you?'

She drew her face away, wincing at the unmistakable contempt in his voice. She was a goddess. She could probe into the secrets of men's minds, and she knew that Shiva had given Chand Saudagar a magic power that could bring dead things back to life.

Chand Saudagar looked contemptuously at Manasa. Then and there he sat down cross-legged in the lotus posture. Controlling his thoughts, his senses, his emotions, and even his very breath, he meditated upon his secret mantra. Manasa, watching him, writhed in anger as, before her eyes, the earth grew green and lush with grass, the flowers began to bloom again, and the birds to sing.

When Chand Saudagar returned to consciousness she was gone. Only her hissing voice lingered in the air and whispered in his heart: 'We shall meet again, Chand Saudagar. I am not so easily thwarted. One day you will bow down and worship me.'

But the next time they met, Chand Saudagar did not know Manasa Devi, for she was in the guise of a beautiful young mortal girl. And the stern merchant prince, husband of many wives, father of many sons and daughters, fell in love with her, and begged her to marry him.

'I will,' replied the girl so softly and shyly that he longed to touch her and feel her reality. But the girl drew back from him and whispered: 'But first you must give me a gift.'

Chand Saudagar cried: 'All I have is yours, my dearest.'

She edged close to him and whispered: 'Is that a promise?'

'Ask what you will and you shall have it,' Chand Saudagar answered in a trembling voice.

'Then teach me the magic spell that brings back the dead to life,' said the girl and Chand Saudagar grew pale. The magic spell could not be divided or shared. If he gave it away he could never have it back. All his life he had treasured it.

'Teach it to me,' wheedled the girl. 'Will you not teach me it?' and she looked lovely as she spoke; her large eyes set his senses swimming.

He began to convince himself: 'She will be my wife. What does it matter whether she keeps the spell or whether I have it? For we will be one when we are married.' Then, looking into her eyes and telling her to listen carefully, he taught her the magic mantra.

She repeated the words, whispering them again and again; and, as she did so, he saw her form change. Before his eyes she rose up in the air, and, in her, he caught a fleeting but unmistakable glimpse of Manasa Devi, Manasa's mocking laughter rang in his ears: 'I have tricked you Chand Saudagar and you have been fooled. Your magic power has gone and your pride has been brought to dust. Bow down and worship me now or worse will come.'

'I have been a fool,' Chand Saudagar admitted sadly to himself, and his hatred and scorn of Manasa Devi increased a hundredfold. He looked at where Manasa had vanished and shook his fists at the empty air;

'Do your worst, Manasa Devi,' he muttered angrily. 'Have I not said so before? But I shall never, never worship you.'

'How obstinate he is,' Manasa said in her heart and she grew the more eager to have him worship her; for she knew that his devotion, once secured, would be unswerving. She marvelled at his steadfastness and, for the first time, felt a flicker of doubt. But it did not last, and the words of the magic mantra leapt alive to her tongue. She laughed remembering how Chand had swallowed the bait. She looked at the garden blooming in loveliness on the earth below, and she blew her poisoned breath over it and chuckled softly, maliciously, to see it reduced to a barren desert.

'I have been a fool,' Chand Saudagar thought to himself again as he saw it happen. 'But I will never allow her to best me a second time.'

Then he remembered his friend Shankara who also knew the magic mantra. He would go to Shankara's house and get the mantra afresh from him.

But Manasa was watchful and her vengeance, far-reaching. 'Ah!' said she. 'Do not think you can outwit me!' She flew to Shankara's house, reaching earlier than Chand did, and struck him dead.

When Chand Saudagar arrived he found his friend gone and his family weeping bitterly for him.

'This is the snake woman's doing!' cried Chand.

But he was powerless, crippled before her wiles and cunning. Mourning his lost friend, he made sorrowfully for home, little knowing what lay ahead. For, when she found him still unyielding, Manasa sent serpents into his mansion. One by one they bit his six sons. As each lay dying, she appeared before the weeping father and demanded worship.

'Do not imagine all this has happened by chance,' she told him. 'I am behind it all.' Her eyes glittered like hard black diamonds. 'You may still save your sons, Chand Saudagar,' she pointed out. 'If you will worship me, I shall give them life.'

But he lifted up his face, wan and grey with sorrow, and in a choking voice cried out: 'Go from here, snake woman, and do what you will. I shall never worship you.'

'We shall pursue this matter to the end,' Manasa said darkly.

A year went by. The time came for Chand Saudagar's ships to put out to sea. Laden with rich cargo, they went sailing over the ocean to distant ports. The merchandise sold at a good profit. All seemed to be going well but, on the homeward voyage, Manasa began to make her presence felt. In mid-ocean a violent storm arose; the black starless sky overhead flashed with lightning. One by one, Chand Saudagar's ships were destroyed, some crashing to pieces on the treacherous rocks, others capsizing and sinking in the dark, stormy sea. When morning came Chand found himself floating on the waters, his cold fingers clutching a piece of wood. He was faint with hunger and thirst. He clung desperately to the wood but, all the while, his fingers were growing numb and his strength was ebbing away. He cried out to Parvati, the wife of Shiva, to come to his help, but he had reckoned without Manasa. She hovered about him as he floated on the waves and would not let Parvati approach the unhappy man. She complained to Shiva, her father:

'Is it not enough for Parvati that she has banished me from heaven? Must she also take from me my hope of worship?'

Shiva saw her point. No it was not fair, he agreed. He told Parvati so and persuaded her to keep out of this conflict.

'Will you not worship me?' Manasa cried out repeatedly. 'Your

124

life is in my hands.'

'No,' gasped Chand Saudagar. 'Never. I would rather die.'

He began to meditate upon death and the god of death, for all hope of life seemed now at an end as he floated upon the dark and endless waters. But a voice whispered, soft and enticing in his ear:

'You are too young to die, Chand Saudagar; life is beautiful. The earth is full of secrets you must discover . . . you are too young, Chand Saudagar, too young to die.'

He knew the voice was Manasa's and he opened his eyes to command her to leave. As he did so, he caught a gleam of light in the distance. He saw a shining object bobbing up and down upon the waves. Chand Saudagar's heart leaped up.

'Parvati has heard my prayer,' he cried, a great hope swelling within him. And suddenly he wanted desperately to live. Suddenly he knew he was going to live.

'Look, snake woman, look there at that shining moon-like object. It draws nearer . . . Parvati has answered my prayer.' Chand Saudagar clung to the piece of wood and struggled to swim so that he would not be swallowed up by the waters.

'Parvati . . . Ha! Parvati—what a fool you are!' Manasa taunted him, but he did not hear her voice, so intent was he on watching the golden object. As it came nearer he saw it was a wonderful, golden throne. Now he was sure the mother goddess had sent it.

'It is a throne for me. Parvati has sent it,' he shouted.

Nearer and nearer came the throne and suddenly it was beside him.

'Goddess, mother, giver of life!' cried Chand Saudagar loudly, and he let go the piece of wood to stretch out for the throne. Then an agonized groan escaped him as he saw that the throne had emblems on it, not of Parvati, but of the snake woman.

Manasa shrieked with laughter, as Chand Saudagar snatched his hand away as if stung.

'Take my help, fool,' hissed Manasa in his ear, 'or you will surely drown today.'

'No,' Chand Saudagar panted, even as the waves closed over him. 'Never will I take your help! I would rather die,' and he sank into unconsciousness.

'It will never do to let him die,' Manasa reflected, 'for it is worship I want, and what worship can a dead man give?' So she kept him alive, and caused him to float upon the waters, until the waves brought him to the shores of a strange country. He was thrown upon the sand and here he lay, unconscious and unmoving, as if dead. A passer-by discovered him and hurried to his aid, and so cleverly did Manasa manipulate fate that this passer-by happened to be a physician. He made the breath return to Chand's lungs and the blood flow in his cold, stiff limbs. Chand Saudagar opened his eyes to find himself in the midst of a crowd of alien people. But they were kindly and hospitable and they brought him food and drink to revive him. One of them, a wealthy and generous citizen named Chandraketu invited him to his house. He gave Chand Saudagar gifts of costly muslin and silk garments and served him rich and delicious foods while attendants sang and danced for him and made him comfortable.

The music crept into Chand Saudagar's blood like a drug. It lulled him into gentle dreams, relaxed his tired limbs, brought him happy thoughts. He lay on his silken couch enjoying the pleasant sensation. His eyes gazed lazily at the painted ceiling above him. It was sculpted with curving, twisting patterns. His eyes followed the patterns. Suddenly he gave a start, as he was jerked out of his dream-world, for he found himself staring into the eyes of a yellow sculpted snake. Instinctively, quickly, he looked away, but he saw how that the whole ceiling was sculpted with snake forms, painted over in bright gaudy yellows, greens and reds. Cobras and pythons, kraits and vipers, rock snakes and sea snakes, water snakes, tree snakes . . . they twisted about each other and seemed to move and coil and uncoil before his eyes. He turned to look upon the walls to avoid the sight, but here too he found himself staring into the eyes of snakes, reptiles that raised monster hoods and swayed, spat their dark and deadly venom, danced, made love, meditated, and prayed.

With a stifled cry Chand Saudagar leaped to his feet. He fled out of the door and into the street. As he went down it, he saw that, at every milestone, there stood a shrine and within it, when he looked inside, was the mark of Manasa, the snake goddess. At that moment the temple bells began to ring and pipes began to play.

'What worship is this?' he asked a passer-by, though he dreaded the answer.

'This city belongs to Manasa Devi,' said the man. 'The people here worship her and her snakes.'

Chand Saudagar was now in a rage. Not a minute longer would he spend in that city. He threw away everything he had been given, even the clothes he wore and then, naked, made his way out of the city gates. And now he was a wanderer, homeless and friendless, and

troubles followed thick and fast, for Manasa Devi, never leaving his side, sent bad luck to dog his footsteps. The village children stoned him and the elders set their dogs on him. Hunger gnawed at his vitals. Once a charitable person took pity on him and gave him a handful of cooked rice to eat. Gratefully, he wrapped the rice in a banana leaf and descended to the riverside to wash. But Manasa caused a rat to come up and devour the rice so that he had to go hungry again. As he gazed sorrowfully at the remains of the now inedible food, he heard the snake woman's familiar, mocking voice:

127

'These things have not happened by chance, Chand Saudagar. Understand that I, Manasa, am behind it all. So at least now worship me and you will be spared.'

But at that, he set his teeth and put his fingers in his ears, to shut out the voice: 'Go from me, Manasa Devi,' he said, stubborn as ever. 'I will have nothing to do with you.'

In answer he heard her silken laughter, and knew his troubles would not end so soon. And he was right, for Manasa took hold of his mind and caused it to become feeble. When a rich farmer taking pity on him employed him as a servant, he kept making foolish mistakes, until his master lost patience. No one knew or guessed that it was all Manasa's doing—that it was she who was making his wits flounder, his hands falter and his tongue utter stupidities. His master beat and abused him, and cuffed his ears. He, who had ruled over a city and been served and obeyed by hundreds of people, had now to suffer worse hardships than a slave. When he remembered his past and compared it with his present condition he could not hold back his tears. But when he was saddest and most down-hearted, then Manasa appeared to him, whispering, coaxing, cajoling, threatening.

'These things have not happened by chance,' she said to him. 'I, Manasa, am the power behind it all, and I will not rest until I have won you over. Even now it is not too late. Offer me worship and I will make all your troubles end.' But he would not yield.

At last one day, unable to bear it any longer, he left his master and went wandering again, until after many weeks he arrived hungry and sore, covered with dust and caked with mud, his clothes hanging in rags on his thin, wasted body, into his native city of Champaka Nagar. Slowly, painfully he made his way home.

Great was the rejoicing in Chand Saudagar's house when the master returned. His family wept with joy and the attendants brought him scented water to wash. Friends came with gifts to greet him, and everywhere prayers were offered to thank the gods for his safe return. It seemed as if his troubles had ended at last. When he recovered his strength, he turned his attention once more to his business, and it began to flourish again. The misfortunes he had suffered seemed to belong to a distant past.

But Manasa Devi had not given up. Although he did not know it, she was awaiting her chance. When, that year, a beautiful boy was born to him and his wife, Manasa crept invisibly into the room and stood by the cradle, smiling her mysterious smile. There was great jubilation in the household at the birth, and the child was given the name of Lakshmindra. Not long afterwards, a girl was born to a merchant in a neighbouring city whom the parents named Behula, and Manasa laughed softly, triumphantly, to herself.

As Behula grew up, the fame of her loveliness spread. Lakshmindra heard about Behula and yearned to have her for his wife. Chand Saudagar, glad of his son's choice, met Behula's father and the marriage of Behula and Lakshmindra was fixed.

But when the astrologers and soothsayers looked into the future, they declared that they saw only evil signs. They predicted that Lakshmindra would die of snake-bite on the night of the wedding. Chand Saudagar trembled and paled. He would have called off the marriage, for he knew that Manasa Devi had not forgiven or forgotten. But Lakshmindra pined for Behula and would not listen to his father. Whatever happened, he said, he would have only Behula for his bride.

So Chand Saudagar decided to outwit Manasa. He sent for the master builder in the country and ordered him to build a steel house for Lakshmindra and Behula. There were to be no openings or cracks in the house at all. Lakshmindra and Behula would spend the first night of the wedding in this steel house and Chand promised the builder a big fortune if he would do this for him.

But Manasa Devi was not so easily countered: 'Fool!' thought she, smiling her grim smile. 'Do you imagine that you can defeat me?'

128

At night she appeared in her terrible snake form before one of the workmen building the house and threatened to destroy him and his entire family, root and branch, if he did not do as she wished. The miserable man, quaking with fear, agreed to obey her and Manasa Devi said: 'I do not ask for much. Leave a tiny crack, thin as a hair, in the corner of the steel wall. That is all. If you obey me you will have rich rewards of money and gold and precious stones, but if you do not, then remember, I can destroy you completely.'

So, when the steel sheets were being joined together, the man left a tiny crack in them, the breadth of a single hair. 'No harm could come of *that*!' he consoled himself. 'No snake could crawl through such a crack.'

Behula and Lakshmindra were married. The ceremonies over, the guests blessed the couple and left. The people of the household retired one by one to sleep. Lakshmindra led his bride to their room in the steel house. It was decked with flowers and there were delicate traditional designs chalked with rice-paste on the floor. A silver vessel of milk stood on a low stool in a corner; Behula had asked for it. Wick lamps burned in niches in the walls and the soft scent of incense filled the air.

Presently the whole house grew quiet, as the inmates went to sleep. Lakshmindra put out the lamps one by one and left only one wick light burning. Then he lay down. He was tired after the many ceremonies and fell asleep at once. But Behula sat on the bed, her eyes open. She looked at the youth she had married and felt a great love stir in her heart at the sight of his beauty. She sat beside him watching and as she watched she wove a rope with quick fingers, murmuring all the while a prayer for her husband's life. Sleep would not come to her; her mind was alert, waiting, all tense and listening.

Suddenly her eyes spotted a swift darting movement in the room. She saw something glide across the floor—a small golden thing, no thicker than a thread, and she drew in her breath as, following it with terror-stricken eyes, she realized that it was a living thing—a snake. As she continued to stare she saw it swell and grow to an enormous size. She saw it settle in a corner, coil on dreadful coil, and it watched her out of its beady eyes, swaying its hood and flicking its thin forked tongue in and out.

Behula glanced at the sleeping youth who was her husband, and all her being cried out to the gods to spare him. Softly she rose from where she sat and taking a bowl of milk she set it on the floor. The snake looked at the bowl. It began to uncoil itself and to creep on its belly towards it. Then she heard it drink the milk. She saw it grow fat and sleepy.

'Come,' Behula whispered to the snake. 'Come, golden creature, come and be tamed.'

The snake's yellow hood swayed menacingly. She heard it hiss. But she held out her hands and spoke to it as one would to a pet dog. 'Draw nearer, pearl of my eyes—come closer.' And the snake obeyed.

Nearer and nearer it crawled until it was only a few spans away from her. In the twinkling of an eye, she slipped over its golden head a noose of the rope she had woven, and made it fast. Now the snake was caught. Death had been trapped. She tethered the snake to the bedpost as if it had been a cow, and returned to her bed to watch.

The moon sailed high in the heavens. Behula began to doze, but only fitfully. At the slightest movement or rustle she would start and wake, and stare wide-eyed into the night. And it was well that she did so, for there came, only a short while afterwards, through the crack in the floor, a second golden thread-like creature. Her blood froze as she recognized a second snake and saw it swell until it became even bigger than the first. Once again, her heart pounding against her ribs, the girl hurried to where the milk was kept, and quickly pouring another bowlful, she set it down for the creature to drink. As the first snake had done, so did the second. It began to lap up the milk and Behula quickly slipped another noose round its neck and tied it up, then went back to her watching. When a third snake came, the girl tied up that one as she had the others.

From the depths of the underworld Manasa watched. She saw how the lovely, clever girl spoilt all her plans. Manasa's eyes grew baleful. She began to utter magic words, and powerful fumes began to fill the room. They wafted over the girl's head, grew thick around her and caused her eyes to grow heavy with sleep, her head to nod. In the silence of the night the girl, tired out with watching, fell asleep at last. And while the young couple slept, a fourth snake came gliding into the room, and swelled to an enormous size. Swiftly it slid up to the sleeping Lakshmindra, struck his ankle and bit him; the poison coursed through the blood; he uttered one cry and then lay very still.

Behula awoke screaming. She saw the great black and gold reptile shrink once more to the size of a thread and glide out through the crack in the steel wall. She looked at her husband. He lay still and blue. Her head swam. Sobs choked her as she realized that all was over—Lakshmindra was dead; she was a widow who had hardly been a bride!

The household came hurrying into the bridal chamber at the sound of her cries, and when they saw the three snakes tied up in a corner, they knew that Lakshmindra had died of snake-bite. They wept and mourned and beat their breasts and tore their hair. But it was, after all, what had been predicted.

Then, according to the custom in that region, by which a man

130

who had died of snake-bite was never burnt, Lakshmindra's body was carried to the riverside, and placed on a raft to be set afloat on the water. Somewhere along the course of the river (people hoped) there might live a holy man or a medicine man or a magician who might see the body and revive it. Crowds of mourners and sightseers had gathered to pay their last respects to the young bridegroom, so cruelly snatched from life.

Behula stood, staring before her as if held by a magic spell. She was not weeping and she seemed not to know that she was among people. For suddenly she moved away from them all, and they saw her walk towards the raft on which the body lay and step upon it and take her seat on it. They saw her lift the dead youth's head on to her lap. They called out to her to come back among them. But she seemed not to hear. It was only when Lakshmindra's mother caught her arm and began to pull her away, that she awoke:

'Do not try to keep me, mother,' she cried out. 'I must go with my husband wherever he goes. I must be with him when he returns to life and opens his eyes.' When the mourners found they could not persuade her, they gave in and went back, sadly, to their homes. Only the old mother-in-law remained by the river-bank, weeping as if her heart would break. As the raft began to float away, Behula called out to her to take heart. 'Tend the wick lamp in the bridal chamber, mother, and keep it filled with oil,' she said, 'for as long as its flame burns, all will be well!' The raft floated down the river, with Behula sitting on it beside the stiff cold body of her husband. Past villages they went, and past towns. Everywhere people stood on the banks and stared at the curious sight. Sometimes the raft drifted ashore and villagers brought her food to eat and water to drink, and when they heard her story, they pitied her and tried to make her give up her resolve. 'He is quite, quite dead!' they told her, looking sadly at the decomposing body, 'You must give him up.' Behula shook her head. She felt within her a power that was stronger than herself, but did not know that it was Manasa Devi urging her not to give up hope. Thus they drifted on, the dead Lakshmindra and his bride, and presently the raft came to the city where Behula's parents lived. All her family came to the river-bank, begging her to stop and come and stay with them.

'Not until my husband's life is restored!' she answered, and the raft went drifting on. The river grew dark now, and sluggish. Crocodiles and water snakes lurking among the weeds surrounded her and threatened to devour her. Behula clasped her hands and

132

began to pray. She knew that it was Manasa Devi who had sent all these troubles upon her, and she cried out to Manasa Devi and begged her protection. Manasa Devi tossed her haughty head. She smiled a triumphant smile. At last a member of Chand Saudagar's family had been overcome! She had won. Manasa Devi extended her hand in answer to the girl's prayer and protected the raft from the dangers of the river.

Six months went by, and one day when the fields were green with newly planted rice, the raft carried Behula and Lakshmindra to a village where, upon the bank, Behula saw a woman washing clothes and hanging them out to dry. A little boy was playing near her, a bright-eyed, lively child full of mischief and childish pranks. Behula saw how he teased and pestered his mother, hindering her in her work. She saw the mother laugh at first and cajole the child, and then frown. She saw her scold the boy for coming in the way. The little fellow did not care. He pranced about like a young colt and pierced the air with his shrill, joyous cries. Behula saw his harassed mother grow angry and shake her finger at her son. The child laughed merrily. Suddenly Behula saw the woman seize the boy and wring his neck. Horror-stricken, she saw the woman lay the boy's limp body on the ground. She felt sick with dread, but held by some hidden power, she continued to look. The woman proceeded calmly with her work until she had finished washing and hanging out all her clothes. Then Behula saw her turn round. She saw her take some water in her hands. She saw her lips move, her body grow rigid. She saw her sprinkle water on the boy's still form. Breathless, the girl continued to stare, and then she saw the boy sit up, alive and healthy, and run back again to his pranks. Behula now knew that the long journey and search were over. She secured the raft to a stump on the river-bank and stepped out. She approached the woman, her timid footsteps guided (though she did not know it) by Manasa's whispered command.

'Who are you?' she asked the woman, who smiled and held out her arms.

'I am Neta, companion of the snake goddess: come with me!' she said and Behula followed.

There was a shrine in a cave, hidden away in the hills, a dark and primitive shrine, deserted and forgotten.

'Seek help within,' said the woman, and Behula entered. At any other time she would have been afraid. But now her love gave her courage. She would do anything to bring her husband back to life.

She looked about her with a pounding heart and as her eyes grew accustomed to the darkness, she saw everywhere the marks of snake worship, and heard invisible fingers pluck at invisible strings to make wild, yearning melodies. Unseen drums throbbed out savage rhythms such as she had never heard before. Cold bodies slithered past her and the girl trembled. But she walked on until she came to the innermost part of the shrine. And there, suddenly, she was face to face with the snake goddess, Manasa. Behula knew her. Had they not met in some dim, forgotten past, long aeons ago? She fell at the snake woman's feet and begged her with tears for her husband's life. Manasa shook her head.

'Not until you promise to win your father-in-law over to me,' she answered.

Behula's lovely eyes clouded over, as she remembered the stubborn old man who was her father-in-law.

'Persuade him?' She quailed at the thought, remembering how he sat cross-legged on his tigerskin before the symbol of Shiva, meditating upon the eternal, caring nothing for the things of the world. How could she, who had neither wisdom nor philosophy nor learning, hope to convert him? But the thought of Lakshmindra lying

still and lifeless on the raft returned, and her eyes began to glow with a strange fire.

'Grant me my husband's life and I will win over my father-in-law to you,' she whispered. The snake woman's lips curled in a smile; her features relaxed. The battle had been a long and dreary one, but she saw it coming to an end at last.

'Lead me to the raft,' she commanded the girl, and when they got there, she crouched by Lakshmindra and gazed at his waxen face. Softly, softly she began to utter strange words of magic, while her whole body swayed with their power and exotic rhythm. To the sound of distant drums and wild pipes she sprinkled charmed water upon him and called his name. Once, twice, three times. At the third call, the eyelids flickered. Then the fingers and toes began to twitch. With a sudden sobbing sound the breath returned; the blood began to trickle into the cold, blue limbs. He moaned, opened his eyes. He sat up and looked about him and Manasa vanished like mist at the touch of sunshine, while her voice echoed all around: 'Remember, Behula. Remember your promise.'

'Why, where are we?' uttered Lakshmindra. Behula smiled unsteadily, eyes brimming, lips quivering. Then she took up the oars

and began to row and the raft went gliding over the sun-spangled waters until it reached Champaka Nagar.

'There are crowds to welcome you,' Behula told her husband, 'and I can see your sisters among them.'

'It's true,' cried the sisters of Lakshmindra as they saw the raft approach. 'Our brother is alive.' They were hysterical with joy and they held out their hands in welcome as the raft touched the shore. But Behula restrained them. 'Not yet,' she said, 'Go and bring your mother here.'

The girls went running to the house and breathlessly related to their mother the strange things they had seen. At first she would not believe them. But then she remembered her daughter-in-law's words about the wick lamp in the bridal chamber. She ran to the steel house and there was the wick lamp, its flame burning, bright and steady and clear. She knew then that Lakshmindra was alive and hurried to the river-bank to welcome him home.

Tears rolled down her wrinkled face at the sight of her beloved son, and she held out her arms to embrace the couple. But Behula, remembering her promise to the snake goddess, held her husband back, and would not let his mother touch him.

'We may not enter the house, dear mother, until Chand Saudagar promises to worship Manasa Devi.' And she told them the story of her great adventure.

'If he loves his son, he cannot hold out any longer,' her mother-in-law answered.

Then she and her daughters went to Chand Saudagar and begged him, with tears flowing down their cheeks, to relent.

'Is your son not dearer to you than your pride?' they cried, and the old man felt himself weaken at last. Long years he had lived by his resolution and he had borne every sorrow and suffering that had come to him. But now the sight of the weeping women was too much for him. And when he thought of Behula, his heart softened.

136

'Very well,' he addressed Manasa Devi, who was invisible but who, he knew was there, hovering about them like a silent bat. 'Very well, Manasa, you shall have my worship!'

The girls began to clap their hands and dance. But Chand Saudagar was a proud and haughty man. He held up his hand and his face grew very stern. 'I have not finished speaking,' he admonished them, and went on: 'It is true, Manasa, that I will offer you worship on the eleventh day of the waning moon. But I shall make my offerings with my left hand, for my right shall ever be faithful to

Lord Shiva. And I shall turn my face away from the image of Manasa when I pray to her.' And he shut his eyes and set his mouth in a grim line.

The girls gasped, and his wife was about to protest. But Chand Saudagar would do no more. Even Manasa Devi had to be satisfied, for she, too, was tired of the long and dreary struggle.

Behula and Lakshmindra entered the house amid song and dance and great rejoicing. They lived long years and were very happy together, but neither forgot what they had gone through. Chand Saudagar offered Manasa Devi worship on the eleventh day of the waning moon each month, but only with his left hand, and with his face turned away. But in the villages on the river-bank, the story of Behula and Lakshmindra spread and was on every tongue. And so, in the month of Shravan (around August) when the earth is green with recent rains and the rivers are full, the festival of Manasa Devi is celebrated in the villages of Bengal. The villagers tell of Manasa and Chand Saudagar and sing of Behula, the beautiful, whose devotion brought her husband back to life.

7

Kacha and Devayani

In days gone by there was continuous war between the gods and the demons or the asuras. Their hatred for each other was fierce and never-ending and not a day passed without fighting between the two. In these wars it was the demons or asuras who always won, for they were stronger—their numbers never decreased. The gods hurled powerful weapons at them and killed many each day and, at sunset, when truce was declared, would go back to their heaven, satisfied that they had killed off most of the enemy. But when morning dawned they would find, to their surprise and dismay, that the demon armies were as powerful as before! All the demons they had killed the previous day would be back in their ranks, alive and strong, and ready once more for battle. And all the while, the gods found their own numbers growing smaller.

'How do they do it?' the gods asked Brihaspati, the sage who was their adviser and teacher. 'You are wise and you ought to know.'

Brihaspati stroked his beard. 'I do know,' he answered thoughtfully. 'It is because of their teacher, the one-eyed Shukracharya. He helps them. Each time a demon is slain, Shukra repeats a magic incantation that brings him back to life.'

The gods looked at Brihaspati in amazement. 'Well then, Brihaspati, why do you not repeat the same incantation and bring our dead to life?'

Brihaspati stood before them, his eyes lowered and his hands folded. He did not know the incantation; he had never learnt it.

The gods were furious. They surrounded him on all sides, threateningly and shouted: 'What kind of teacher are you then? We feed you, clothe you and pay you handsomely, and you tell us you are powerless before our enemy. The gods die every day in battle and you can do nothing about it . . . .'

They drew closer menacingly. 'Listen, old man,' they said. 'If you do not find a way to defeat the asuras, we shall drive you out of heaven . . . do you hear?'

Brihaspati heard. He knew that the gods meant what they said. Tears ran down his cheeks, and he wrung his hands in terrified despair. 'I must think of a way,' he cried to himself. 'I must somehow get the magic incantation from Shukra.' But he knew this was easier said than done. The asura kingdom was heavily guarded, and Shukra was wily and clever. He would not part easily with the secret incantation.

Brihaspati moved to the window of his room and looked out at the green fields of heaven. It was beautiful country, rich and fruitful. If the gods drove him out, he would have to leave all this and wander penniless in the cruel world. 'That must not happen,' muttered Brihaspati to himself. 'I will not let it happen. I must find some way to gain possession of that incantation.'

His clever mind began to hatch plan after plan, till suddenly an idea occurred to him. 'Why didn't I think of this before?' he said, happily.

Brihaspati called a servant to him. 'Go bring my son Kacha to me,' he said. 'Tell him the matter is urgent and he must come immediately.' When Kacha came, Brihaspati ordered the servant to leave them.

'Kacha, my son,' said Brihaspati. 'I need your help.'

'You have only to say the word, father,' answered Kacha, 'and I shall obey.'

Brihaspati told Kacha all that had happened. 'You must go down to the demon kingdom, my son, and somehow find out the magic incantation. Otherwise the gods will drive me out of heaven . . . .'

Kacha's eyes began to shine with excitement. 'Do not be afraid, father,' he said. 'By fair means or foul, I shall get it for you. Shall I start at once?'

Brihaspati gripped his arm. 'Wait,' he admonished. 'You will have to be very careful. You will be alone in enemy country, and the asuras are cunning. If they discover your presence, they will stop at nothing . . . .'

'I am not afraid,' said Kacha. But the old man continued: 'It is not enough to be brave. You must be cunning. You must go in disguise, so that they do not know you. You must then persuade Shukra to accept you as his disciple, and you must stay with him and learn all that he has to teach. You must be watchful and patient and keep your wits about you. And you must make use of every chance to gain your end. It will not be easy, Kacha, for the demons will watch you with their millions of eyes.'

Kacha bent down and touched his father's feet: 'Bless me, father, and wish me well,' he said. 'I shall not return home without the magic spell.'

Then, taking a few of his possessions tied in a small bundle, the boy set out on his mission. Down the starlit path of heaven he went, over the earth and across the oceans, until he came to the country of the asuras.

Kacha walked swiftly. Over the hills and valleys of demonland he walked, and through its cities and villages. And the asuras stared at him and wondered where he had come from and who he was. 'You are a stranger in this country,' they said. 'What do you seek here?'

'I am a brahmin from the world of mortals,' Kacha answered. 'I have travelled far, good demons, to become a pupil of the famed teacher, Shukra. Can you show me the way to his house?'

The demons looked at him suspiciously. 'How do we know he's telling the truth?' they asked each other. So they misled him and caused him to lose his way several times through the forests and the rocky mountain paths. They caused him to slip and fall and bruise himself. They placed a hundred obstacles in his path. Snakes and wild animals appeared where none had existed, landmarks he had seen vanished mysteriously even as he walked; bridges were washed away before his very eyes, and great columns of fog rose up again and again and hid the landscape from his sight. Fearful storms arose, and once his passage was delayed when the rains caused a great landslide, bringing great boulders crashing down the mountainside.

But he was brave and determined, and young and strong, and he persisted, never losing heart. Morever, there were many kind people who helped him, offering him food and shelter and putting him on the right path and giving him correct directions, so that after many days of travelling, Kacha came at last to a small green valley. By now he was tired and footsore. He wondered if the demons had tricked him again, and he had lost his way.

It was a very lovely spot with flowering trees and a little brook singing a song as it flowed over the pebbles, and the grass was soft and fragrant under his feet. Kacha sat down under a tree, and the breeze brought him a shower of petals from the branches above and lulled him to sleep, blowing gently about him.

And as he slept, there collected around him a group of demon girls. They were taking a walk in the woods and playing hide-and-seek, when one of them saw the stranger and called softly to the others to come and see.

'Look what I've found,' she called.

'It's a boy . . . who could he be?' whispered the second.

'He's a stranger,' observed the third. 'We've never seen him before . . . .'

They tiptoed up to him, and stood staring down at him. Only one of them, Devayani, said nothing. She was the daughter of Shukra, and as she looked at Kacha's young face, it seemed to her that he was the handsomest boy she had ever seen in all her life.

'I wonder who he is?' Devayani whispered to herself. 'I wonder where he's going?'

Just then Kacha opened his eyes, and all the girls fled—all except Devayani. She stayed where she stood and she smiled at him. Kacha arose and joined his hands in greeting.

'I am looking for the house of the great teacher, Shukracharya,' he said. 'Do you know where it is?'

Devayani smiled and answered, 'I do, for Shukracharya is my father. Come, I shall lead you to our house.'

'Why,' thought Kacha, 'surely I am in luck . . . and now begins my adventure!'

Devayani led Kacha to her father and said to him: 'You must accept him as your disciple, father, please, you must.'

Shukra was not so sure. He looked at Kacha out of his one eye and thought: 'Now who could this young fellow be? Why has he travelled all this long, long way to be my pupil? Surely it couldn't be as simple as all that?'

And the demons came round him, squinting their little eyes and nudging each other and whispering: 'We don't like the look of the boy at all. Be careful, great master, perhaps he's an enemy.'

'Nonsense!' snapped Devayani. 'Be off with you, you nasty old men.' She thought of Kacha's long-lashed eyes and his dark wavy hair, and begged: 'Please, father, please don't send him away.' She begged so hard that Shukra yielded.

142

'Well, he does seem to be a pleasant young man,' said Shukra. 'And what harm could he do to us now? Perhaps the demons are too suspicious.' And he agreed to take Kacha as his pupil. Kacha was to stay in the master's house and serve him, as disciples of those days were expected to.

So early each morning Kacha gathered twigs for fuel and for the sacrificial fires. He collected flowers for worship and fetched water. He tended the trees and took the cows to pasture. In return Shukracharya instructed him.

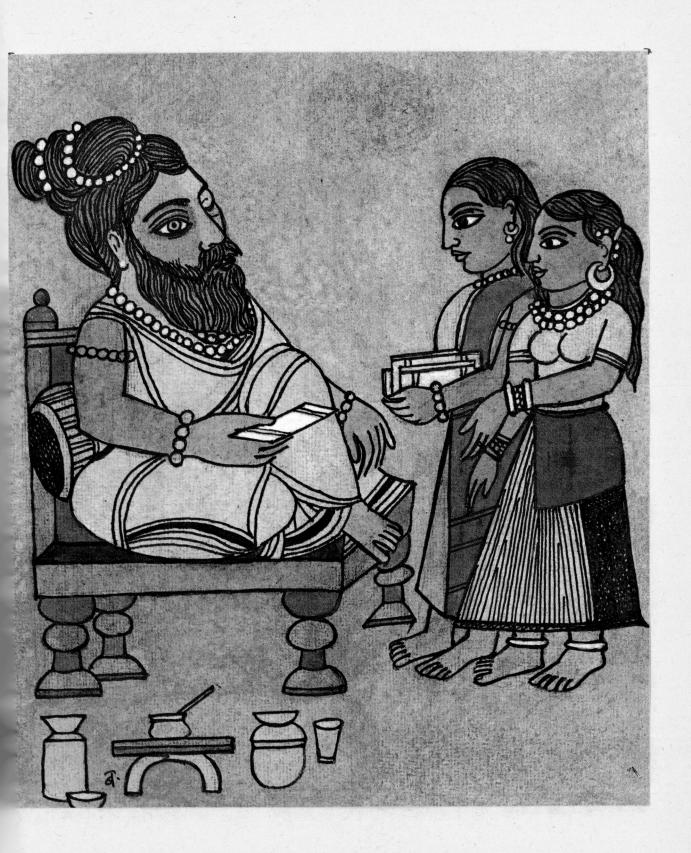

Whenever Kacha was not working or studying Devayani would come running to him, and the two would spend their time together by the brook or under the trees. They went for long walks by the hillside and they watched the moon rise over the lake. Kacha could sing and play and do a thousand things that could delight the heart of a young girl. With each passing day, Devayani became increasingly fond of Kacha until she grew to love him so much that she could do nothing but think of Kacha and dream of him all day long. She had quite lost her heart to the handsome stranger.

But Kacha did not care for Devayani as much as she cared for him. He was always pleasant to her, and he continued to be a good and amusing companion, but never, for one moment, did he forget that he had come to this country to discover the closely guarded secret of the magic incantation that brought the dead to life. That was his goal.

One-eyed Shukra wasn't quite sure about his disciple. He liked the boy. He was well-mannered and diligent, quick to learn and clever at everything. And yet, Shukra wasn't too sure . . . .

And all the while the asuras watched with their million, million eyes and they followed Kacha about, silently, wherever he went. They did not like strangers. They did not trust strangers. 'These are times of war,' they muttered. 'One cannot be too careful.'

Then one day they decided that it would be best to kill Kacha, before he could do them any harm. So they went into their secret hiding places, their deep dark holes, and there they whispered and plotted and schemed for days together, and when they were ready with their plan, they came out again, and went about their tasks with innocent expressions on their demon faces . . . . And all the while they waited for a chance.

One evening, when Kacha went out to the lonely woods to tend his teacher's cattle, the demons seized their opportunity. They lay in wait for him, and they fell upon him and killed him. They tore his body to pieces and threw the pieces to the jackals and the wolves. Then, pleased with their horrible deed, they returned home.

But they had forgotten about Devayani. All day she waited for Kacha. Towards lamp-lighting time when the cows came home to be milked, Kacha was not with them. Devayani began to feel very uneasy.

She crept out of her father's hermitage in search of him, and walked towards the forests, where Kacha took the cattle to graze. 'Kacha,' she called, 'Kacha, where are you?'

But there was no answer. Only the wind howled in the trees and a night bird flew past her, screeching.

'Kacha, Kacha!' she called and called until she knew at last that it was in vain. Fearing for his life, Devayani came running back to Shukra. 'Father,' she cried, 'the night has come and the cows have returned home, but Kacha is not with them. I have searched everywhere for him . . . I fear the demons have killed him. Please, father, you must bring him back to me, for I cannot live without him.'

Shukra said: 'Perhaps he is dead, Devayani. Perhaps the demons have killed him. Whatever has happened, has happened, my child, and all things happen for the best.'

At that Devayani began to weep: 'Father, bring Kacha back to me! Bring him back.'

'If he's dead that's the end of him, my child,' Shukra told her. 'You must forget him, Devayani.'

'It isn't the end,' sobbed Devayani. 'Father, you have the secret that restores the dead to life. Use it to restore Kacha, for if you don't, I shall surely die.'

'It's a very secret and sacred incantation,' began Shukra. 'It must not be lightly uttered . . . .' And he was very reluctant.

But Devayani wept and begged and pleaded so hard that in the end he gave way. He closed his eyes in deep concentration, and chanting the mantras, he called out to Kacha to come. And the next minute Kacha stood before them, smiling and unharmed.

'Why, where have you been, Kacha?' asked Devayani. 'Oh, how I have missed you!'

Kacha told them how the asuras had killed him and thrown his body to the wolves and jackals.

'But now you have come back,' Devayani said happily, 'and that is all that matters.'

The asuras gnashed their teeth with rage when they saw Kacha restored. They were determined to try again.

So another day, when Kacha had gone out into the forest, they followed him again and fell upon him. And this time they ground his body to a paste and mixed it with the waters of the ocean. They thought they had been very successful this time. But it wasn't really quite as clever an idea as they imagined. Because, when Kacha did not return home, Devayani guessed that the demons had been up to some new malice, and she went up to her father again, begging him to help her.

'If he's dead, I'll kill myself,' she threatened, and she neither ate nor drank nor slept, but wept all day and night for her beloved friend, until Shukra agreed to restore Kacha to life. He closed his eyes, and concentrated on the magic words, and called out to Kacha, who came out of the ocean bed, shining-eyed and smiling; not a hair on his head had come to harm.

'We have failed again,' growled the demons, and they tore their hair in rage. They decided that they must do something really drastic since Kacha could not be killed in the ordinary way.

'He's no ordinary mortal, as he pretends to be,' they muttered to each other. 'Perhaps he is a spy from the country of the gods come to steal our secret weapons . . . . Perhaps he has come among us to steal Shukra's magic incantation.'

And when they said that, they wondered why it had not occurred to them before. Of course it was that! The boy Kacha had come to steal the magic incantation. 'Well, if we don't kill him, he'll kill us,' cried the demons. And all day long and all night long they plotted and schemed darkly . . . but they knew that all their plans would be foiled by Devayani. At last one of them, who was brighter than the rest, thought of a way, by which they could get rid of Kacha once and for all.

'Let's kill him and burn his body,' said he, his eyes glinting wickedly. 'Let's mix the ashes in wine, and give it to Shukra to drink; you know how Shukra loves wine. He will drink it all up, for Shukra is a slave to drink even more than he is a slave to his daughter . . . . And Kacha will never be able to come out of Shukra's body without tearing open his stomach. And if his stomach is torn, then Shukra will die . . . and surely Devayani would not want her father to die, would she?'

'No, she wouldn't,' chortled the asuras together. And they

shouted with joy and hugged each other and danced their wild dances in great glee.

The next day they followed Kacha as they had done before, and they killed him. They burnt his body, collected the ashes, mixed them in a wine which they had brewed, then they brought the wine to Shukra, saying: 'This is a very special wine,' and they held out the container to him. Shukra, who suspected nothing, took it and drank it all up. Wine was his weakness. 'It is excellent wine,' he observed, as he savoured it. 'You're very clever to have made it.'

And the demonfolk chuckled to themselves.

When twilight fell, Devayani waited for Kacha's return. All day her thoughts had been with him. She had sat under a tree and woven flower garlands for him. She had thought of a new game to play. 'Perhaps he has a new story to tell me,' she thought, 'or he might have a new song to sing.' They would go out into the woods and see the glow-worms in the trees. Life had become very joyful for Devayani since Kacha had come. She hoped one day to be his wife . . . . But here her face clouded over, and she grew sad. Why was it that Kacha did not seem to care for her as much as she cared for him? He was always friendly, amusing and kind . . . but she was not special to him as he was to her.

'Never mind,' thought Devayani. 'I'll win his love before long.'

And then she looked up at the night sky, and she saw that all the stars were twinkling.

'Why, it's very late and Kacha hasn't come back!' she cried anxiously. 'Oh, what could have happened?'

She went running to her father, and she began to tell him about her fears. But Shukra was drunk . . . . As she spoke she saw that her father wasn't listening at all. He was in a world of his own, and not quite steady on his feet.

'Father, father,' cried Devayani, and the tears streamed down her cheeks. 'Listen, father, please listen to me.'

It was a long time before Shukra understood what his daughter was trying to tell him. 'What?' he said at last, 'Kacha not back?'

'Yes!' Devayani told him. 'It is past midnight and Kacha has not come home. I fear the asuras have killed him.'

At this Shukra tried to tell his daughter how futile it was to bring Kacha back to life. 'The asuras hate him, my child,' he said. 'They will pursue him relentlessly until they destroy him. They will not let him live.'

Devayani did not hear him at all. She was weeping and sobbing, crying out: 'Kacha! Kacha!'

Shukra tried again. 'You are young and beautiful, Devayani. Surely there will be suitors for your hand, richer and more handsome than this unknown youth!'

But Devayani cried, 'Kacha, Kacha!' and was inconsolable.

Then Shukra tried to philosophize, saying, 'Death is only a continuation of life, my child . . . . Indeed there is neither life nor death. All is illusion.' Devayani wept even harder, crying, 'Kacha was no illusion . . . . He was real, and my pain is real too . . . .'

'Very well, then,' said Shukra. 'I shall use the magic incantation and restore him to life, but be sure, the asuras will get him again. So it won't be of much use.'

Devayani began to smile. 'How kind you are, dear father,' she breathed. 'You are the kindest father in the whole world.'

Shukra closed his eyes and sat down assuming the lotus posture. He closed his eyes. His whole body grew very still. His mind spun around like a whirlpool, until every thought was drawn into its vortex and destroyed all except the one thought—the thought of Kacha, whom he must call and restore to life.

'Kacha,' he called in the silence of the night, 'Kacha, come back from the dead, come back from the dead.' And then in low, solemn tones he recited the secret incantation, making the suitable ritual gestures. 'Kacha, come back. Come back from the dead!'

Devayani waited, breathless. She looked all around her. 'Kacha,' she whispered, 'Kacha, my dear Kacha, come back from the dead. Come back.'

Minutes passed. In the sky the stars revolved and changed their positions.

'Why isn't he here, father?' cried Devayani. 'Has the incantation failed? Why does he not answer?'

Shukra looked at his daughter; and there was a puzzled look on his face. 'I can hear his answering voice,' he said. 'He is somewhere near, very, very near. He has, in answer to the mantra, woken from the dead . . . but where is he?'

'Call again, father,' Devayani suggested.

And Shukra called: 'Where are you, Kacha? I hear you near me, but I cannot see you. Why do you not come?' Father and daughter strained their ears to listen.

And suddenly, they heard Kacha's voice: 'Teacher, I am here inside your stomach!'

'Inside my stomach?' cried Shukra in astonishment. 'How did you get there, boy?'

And Kacha told him what the demonfolk had done, and how Shukra had drunk him up with the wine they had given him.

'Those demons!' spluttered Shukra wrathfully. 'So that's the trick they played on me, is it? Wait till I get my hands on them . . . .'

'Father,' cried Devayani, 'what are we going to do about Kacha? You are not going to let him stay in your stomach forever, are you?'

'Oh, no,' Shukra answered, 'it isn't very comfortable, child.'

'No, it isn't,' came Kacha's voice.

'What shall we do?' worried Shukra, holding his stomach with both hands. And Devayani clung to her father, crying: 'Bring Kacha back, father. Please bring him back!'

'From inside my stomach?' asked Shukra. 'Well, there is a

problem there, Devayani.'

She gulped and looked at him now, inquiringly, and Shukra went on:

'Listen, child, Kacha will have to rip open my stomach to come out into the world, and if he does that then I die. And if Kacha remains inside my body then he will die.'

Devayani shook her head slowly.

'One of us must die,' Shukra told her, 'if the other is to live.'

'What shall we do?' cried Devayani.

'Well,' Shukra answered, 'you must choose which of us shall die so that the other may live. Whom will you choose Devayani—your father or the boy you love?'

Devayani was in a terrible dilemma. 'Oh, what shall I do?' she wept. 'Whom shall I choose? Father, you are both equally dear to me . . . How can I choose?'

'But you must, my dear,' Shukra answered gently, 'and you must not waste time. If you delay, you might be too late to save either of us and both may die!'

Devayani saw that her father was right. She began to think. And suddenly, in a flash the answer came to her. 'I have it, father,' she cried to him, 'I know what you must do.' He turned to her puzzled, and she went on: 'Listen, Kacha must come out of your body. And when he does, you will die. But you need not die. Teach him the secret incantation that restores the dead to life, and then, when he comes out of your body, he will be able to bring you back from the dead!'

Shukra stared at his daughter with admiration in his one eye. 'Why, what a clever girl!' he murmured.

But she cried out impatiently: 'Father, hurry up and teach Kacha the incantation.'

So Shukra sat down again and drew all his thoughts together so that his body grew rigid and tense as a drawn bowstring. And then he called out to Kacha and asked him to listen with complete attention. And he taught Kacha, who was inside his stomach, the magic incantation.

At the end of the lesson, Kacha, at Shukra's command, ripped open his teacher's body, and stepped out of it, alive and well. But Shukra lay dead, bleeding, on the earth.

Kacha blinked in the sunshine and looked about him. Once more he had come back from the dead. He felt the warm blood tingle in his veins. He saw the light on the leaves, and heard the birds sing.

The fragrance of flowers was around him, and he felt, with a great wonder, the touch of the earth under his feet.

'How good it is to be alive,' he exclaimed. And then he saw his teacher's body and remembered what he must do. So he sat down, as Shukra had taught him to sit, brought his thoughts together with deep concentration and then uttered the magic incantation. 'Shukra, my teacher, my guru,' he called. 'Come back! Come back from the dead!'

Shukra's torn bleeding body stirred. His eyelids began to flutter. He gave a great groan, and he sat up.

'He's alive!' cried Devayani, her eyes shining with joy. 'My father's alive . . . and Kacha is alive too.'

But she did not rejoice for long.

For now, that Kacha had learnt the incantation, his purpose was served, and he prepared to go home. Devayani stared incredulously at him when he announced his intention.

'It's not true,' she told herself. 'We love each other . . . He can't be serious.' But when she saw him bend down and touch her father's feet, and when she saw Shukra give the boy his blessing, she knew he was. He was not going to stay a day longer with them than was necessary. Her heart cried out: 'How could he, oh, how could he do this to us?'

'Goodbye, dear Devayani,' said Kacha, 'goodbye and god bless you . . . .' And he turned to go. But Devayani looked him straight in the eye, and answered: 'I am going with you, Kacha. I love you . . . I have loved you from the day I first saw you . . . I cannot live without you, and I will have no one else but you for my husband. I will be your wife. I will walk with you to the farthest ends of the earth.'

Kacha frowned. He did not like this at all. Somewhere deep inside him his conscience pricked him:

'Are you sure you've done right, Kacha?' a small voice whispered. 'You knew what you were doing, didn't you, when you allowed Devayani to grow fond of you? You knew you would never marry her, but would go your way to the country of the gods. But still you made use of her to gain your end, didn't you? And now that you've got what you came for, it doesn't matter to you that you have caused her pain . . . that she weeps for you . . . that she will be lonely without you and will shed many tears.'

Kacha bit his lip. He felt very uncomfortable, and he didn't like the voice of his conscience at all. He felt sorry for Devayani. During the long, lonely days when he was away from home, she had kept him company. and helped him forget his loneliness. She had given him many hours of happiness. And she had saved him from death. Three times she had saved him, and the third time she had got for him the precious incantation he had come for. If it had not been for her, Shukra would never have given it to him. He was grateful to her, he *was*, but marriage—that was different. Kacha thought of all the lovely girls he knew in heaven, and it seemed to him that Devayani was very plain indeed.

He thought quickly, for he must get out of this predicament, before it became too awkward and difficult. 'In the holy books it is written,' said Kacha, 'that a disciple is like a son to his teacher. Therefore, Devayani, I am like a son to Shukra. That makes you my sister.' His eyes moved quickly as another thought came to him: 'And I am more than ever Shukra's son, for I have lived inside his body and he has three times given me life. How can I marry you, Devayani, you, who are my sister?'

But Devayani did not hear him at all. She was sobbing her heart out. Shukra put his arm around her and he let her weep. There was little else he could do. 'Perhaps one day the wound will heal,' he said and he turned to look at Kacha.

But Kacha was not there. He had slipped away. He was already speeding heavenwards, the magic incantation safe inside his clever little head.

152

8

Ruru and Pramadvara

Ruru, son of the sage Pramati, was a carefree young man, full of fun and laughter; and he loved a girl called Pramadvara. Unnoticed by her, Ruru watched Pramadvara one day, playing with her companions outside her foster-father's cottage. As he looked at her, it seemed to the young Ruru that he had never before seen anything as lovely as this girl, with her long-lashed eyes and slender limbs. He fell in love with her and, going home, begged his parents for permission to marry her.

Pramati spoke to Sthulakesha, the girl's father, but the latter hesitated, for Pramadvara was an adopted child. Would Pramati, he wondered, accept her as his daughter-in-law? Many years before, Sthulakesha, at prayer in the forest, had heard an infant's cry. He had followed the sound and discovered a child among the reeds of the river, a baby girl, shining in beauty like a small bright star. She stopped crying when she saw the old man; she began to smile and to kick her plump legs. When the baby stretched out her arms to him, Sthulakesha could resist her no longer. He picked her up, brought her home to his family and cared for her like his own daughter. No one knew who her real parents were, though it was whispered that her mother was Menaka, a ravishing dancer at Indra's court. Sthulakesha faced Pramati squarely: 'Well, will you still have this girl for your son's wife?'

Pramati was distressed. His family was descended from the mighty sage Bhrigu, and their blood was pure and without blemish. Now his son wanted a courtesan's daughter, a foundling, for his wife. What was he to do?

But the boy Ruru had no such misgivings. He loved Pramadvara with all his heart, and declared that he would marry no one but her, if she would have him. So Pramati relented, and the day was fixed for the wedding. Ruru waited, restless and impatient for the hour.

But fate had ordained differently. Even as the preparations were being made for the marriage, Pramadvara was bitten by a snake. She stepped on it accidentally in the grass, and in the next moment the snake reared its head and struck her. Pramadvara screamed, and fell. Her frightened companions took one look and ran to tell her family. They came running at the frantic cries only to find their gentle child close to death. It was a fearful sight. Her lovely face was contorted, her lips were blue, her mouth was foaming and her eyes rolled wildly. All efforts to revive her were in vain and, when Ruru arrived there a little while later, Pramadvara was dead.

Pramadvara's family, the neighbours and her companions sat

around the body weeping silent tears. As Ruru approached they made way for him to pass. He knelt beside her on the earth. How still she lay; as if she was sleeping! The agony and the pain were over, the poison had done its foul work and, as if ashamed of its deed, had slipped away leaving no trace; and all her beauty had returned to her. In death she seemed lovelier than she had ever been in life. Ruru gazed and gazed at her. Then suddenly he stood up and ran, for he could not bear to see her so still and white, so far away, where no one and nothing—not even his passionate love—could reach her. His heart ached and his eyes burned with welling tears. He had to be alone with his sorrow and with the thought of his beloved.

Ruru ran into the forest where the trees grew dark and thick, and

there he wept for the girl he loved. His friends came to him begging him to return, but he would not go with them. He shouted at them to let him be. And they had to return dejected to their homes.

Ruru remained in the forest, utterly desolate, and mad with grief. His cheeks grew hollow, his eyes took on a glazed look, and his hair hung, matted and uncombed, on his shoulders. The soles of his feet cracked and bled, and his clothes were in tatters. He wandered aimlessly, heedless of the blazing sun, the icy winds or the driving rain.

At night he lay under the trees and stared with vacant unseeing eyes at the moon and the stars above. When he grew hungry he tore at the earth to find roots for himself and plucked berries or picked fruit that had fallen to the ground. But Ruru was unaware of what he did. His sorrowing heart only remembered Pramadvara, forgetting all else. He saw her everywhere—as a reflection in a river, as a cloud in the sky, as a shape made of mist. Again and again, his family and his friends begged him to return: 'Pramadvara is dead, Ruru, and the wise do not grieve over death, for it is inevitable. Come back, and we shall find you a girl far more beautiful than she was.' But he would not listen and ran away from them, deeper into the forest. And there he wandered alone, weeping.

But after a while his mind slowly began to go over the cause of her death. It was a snake that had cut her off in the fullness of youth. He imagined it over and over again—the young girl at play . . . the snake slithering in the grass . . . the treacherous flash of the golden hood . . . His mind overflowed with images. They changed grief into anger and anger into hatred, until a single thought began to govern his mind—the thought of revenge. He who had been a gentle, laughter-loving boy, was now possessed with the desire to destroy the entire race of the enemy who had taken away his loved one and his happiness.

So it was that Ruru became a hunter and slayer of snakes. He wandered in the wilderness, armed with rocks and stones and sticks, looking for reptiles, and when he found them he killed them with savage yells of triumph. And when he had killed, he felt, for a while, as if some dreadful hunger within him had been satisfied. But only for a while, for very soon his memories tortured him again, and the more he killed, the greater grew his desire to kill. So Ruru let loose the demons of terror in the beauty and peace of the forest, and the snakes fled in fear at his coming.

One day, just as he was about to kill a snake, the reptile cried out in a human voice: 'Do not kill me, I pray you, for I am not a poisonous creature. I am a harmless snake, living out my days in the forest.'

Ruru stopped short; but the next minute his anger returned: 'Wretched one,' he snarled. 'Are you trying to turn me from my purpose? Why do you assume a false human voice? Or have you made me mad? Am I imagining all this?' He crouched low and began to move towards the creature, hissing menacingly: 'Know and understand, evil thing! Ruru is the destroyer of snakes—not their saviour!'

And he would have crushed the snake's head with the stone in his hands if it had not cried out again: 'Believe me, Ruru, I am no snake at all. My name is Dundubha. Listen to me, I implore you.'

Ruru's hand faltered and the reptile glided swiftly away and slipped under a rock. The stone dropped from Ruru's hand, and he uttered a cry of disappointment and rage. But he would not give up, for he had sworn to himself that he would destroy every snake he came across. He tried to look under the rock, and reach the creature with a stick. But the voice continued: 'I was human once like you, Ruru. I too was full of laughter and fun . . . that was my undoing.'

'What does all this mean?' thought Ruru. 'What have I to do with

a snake? Are snakes not my mortal enemies?' But the creature spoke on, in a persuasive voice, and Ruru was forced to listen.

'One day,' said the snake, 'in mischief, I wove a life-like snake of grass, and threw it in the path of a sage. It gave him a fright, as I had intended, and I roared with laughter at his discomfiture. But the sage did not laugh. He was livid with rage and his eyes blazed with anger as he cursed me: "May you change into just such a snake as you made!" he cried. "May you become a reptile crawling in the grass, feeding on frogs and rats and mice."

'Hiding behind a tree, I began to tremble, as I heard that fearful curse. I felt my head and body shrink, my limbs dissolve, the blood in my body turn cold. I found myself gliding up the tree; moving on my belly towards the forked branch in swift, smooth curves. The angry words continued. I began to weep, for my heart and my feelings were still human. I slithered down the tree-trunk again and lay at his feet and pleaded dumbly for forgiveness and mercy. The sage was still dancing wildly in his rage. He could neither hear me nor see me. But after a while he grew calmer and began to call out my name. But I could not reply. He grew uneasy and began to search for me. Suddenly he saw the snake I had become. He gasped with horror, realizing what he had done. Remorse swept over him. He knelt down and picked me up and looked into my eyes. I was still trying, dumbly, to tell him it was only a joke I had played . . . foolish perhaps, but not wicked or malicious. Would he, for that, condemn me to live like this for ever?

'For a long while remorse kept him silent, and then at last he said: "I have wronged you terribly, Dundubha, but what has happened cannot be undone. A curse once uttered cannot be wiped out. I should have thought of that before I spoke. Now I can only repair part of the damage I have done you. I can bless you, my friend, and soften the effect of my cruel, unthinking curse." He raised his right hand and stroked my poor snake-head, saying: "May your life as a snake be only for a short while . . . . May you one day emerge from your prison and become human once again."

' "When?" I pleaded with my eyes. "When will that be? Will you not give me a sign so that I shall know?"

'He answered: "It shall be on the day that you meet Ruru . . . that day shall be the day of your deliverance. You shall become human again." Then he bent down and let me go.

'This is my story,' concluded the snake, Dundubha. 'The day that I meet Ruru is to be the day of my deliverance.'

Ruru who had been listening, rapt, now stared: 'Are you . . . are you . . . is it of me that you speak?' he stammered. He stared at the reptile which had emerged from under the rock and lay coiled now at his feet. At the sight of it, the hatred he had for a brief while forgotten came welling up in his heart once again. And a voice in his head cried: 'A snake is not to be trusted . . . never . . . never . . . . Kill it before it escapes, kill, kill, kill.' He reached out, tottering, but it was too late. While hesitating, he had lost the advantage and now, even as he contemplated the action, a strange and miraculous transformation took place. Where the reptile had been, there now stood a holy sage.

'What . . . what has happened?' gasped Ruru. Then he let out a scream of anger, realizing that his enemy had escaped his wrath. He advanced towards Dundubha with his fists clenched menacingly: 'Sage . . . what have you done? Where is the snake I was going to kill? Speak or I shall kill you.'

The sage smiled. He looked fearlessly into Ruru's wild eyes and something in his look made Ruru hesitate, muttering darkly. 'Your mind is clouded with anger, Ruru,' said the sage, 'and with thoughts of revenge and hatred.'

'Have I not ample cause?' sobbed Ruru.

The sage sat by him. 'Anger will cure nothing, my son,' he said. It will only destroy you. You are descended from a family of ascetics. Will you forget your ancestry and allow your passions to rule you? To give way to grief and to give way to anger are both wrong.'

Ruru listened. But in his misery he could accept nothing the sage was saying. He covered his face with his hands and from time to time moaned: 'I have been wronged—grievously wronged, and a snake has wronged me. How can I forgive the vile creatures of that race?'

Dundubha continued to speak, while above them the birds chirped and called and the squirrels chittered, their tails bobbing up and down. He spoke to him of the code by which wise men live: 'Kindness of heart, forgiveness and love—these are a wise man's guiding stars,' he said.

158

Ruru looked up. 'Love!' he repeated. 'Did you say love?' and he began to laugh mirthlessly. 'There was a time, when I had only love in my heart. I hurt no one, and wished no one evil. And yet this happened to me. Is it any wonder that now my heart burns? Is it any wonder that I feel there is no justice except the justice a man must wrest for himself? Nature is cruel and man must be cruel in turn. He must destroy if he is to survive.'

He began to imagine all over again the death of Pramadvara. Through the torment of his memory he heard the wise man speak once more: 'Nature seems cruel, yes,' said Dundubha, 'and creatures prey on each other and the strong seem to destroy the weak. But these things are part of nature's law. Behind this play of forces is a wonderful order, a plan, a design—a mystery that men will understand if only they open their eyes and their hearts. Behind it all they will see how nature's creatures, the greatest and the smallest, depend on each other and help maintain creation and its balance.'

Ruru listened to him. He could make nothing of his words, but his voice was soothing. When evening came he allowed Dundubha to lead him to a small hut among the forest trees. His steps were heavy as if his feet had been tied to leaden weights.

'Stay with me,' said the kindly Dundubha, and brought him food and clean water to drink. Ruru stayed, because it was the same to him whether he did or did not. He ate and drank what the sage gave him, and slowly his ravaged body grew strong again with the nourishing food. But he still wept inwardly thinking of his Pramadvara.

Every day, Dundubha spoke to the unhappy boy. He led him out into the forest and pointed out to him its glory, its mystery and beauty. But Ruru was like one in a dream, waking to life only when a snake crossed their path. At the sight of a snake he sprang up like lightning to kill it. But Dundubha was quicker than he, and saved the creatures from Ruru's anger.

'Why do you save these evil, venomous creatures?' cried Ruru angrily, and Dundubha answered:

'Because life is a precious gift and no man may destroy what he cannot create.'

Sometimes he answered: 'Because snakes are like you and me, part of god's creation.' But very often he replied simply: 'They are beautiful things—snakes—and it is a sin to destroy beauty.'

'I do not understand at all,' said Ruru.

'Look, my son,' Dundubha whispered. 'If you open your eyes and your heart then you will understand.'

And he pointed out to him the bees and the butterflies gathering honey and scattering pollen and seed. He showed him the secret hiding places where the fish spawned. He showed him the insects and their gleaming rainbow-tinted wings. He pointed out to him the ways of the snail, the tortoise and the earthworm burrowing inside

160

the soil. Following that pointing finger Ruru saw the eagles in their glory reaching for the sun, and the graceful flight of herons and wild ducks.

For quite a while Ruru saw only with his eyes. His heart was hard and unfeeling inside him. But one day he smiled. He smiled to see the deer leap about in the glade; he smiled to see the ducks waddle towards the pond. Smilingly, he sniffed the fragrance of wild flowers. Dundubha's heart rejoiced, for he knew now that the boy's spirit had been healed. He watched over him, observing his every move. And when, one day, he saw him thrill to the beauty of a snake's swaying hood, he knew that the healing was complete. Never more would the boy wander wild-eyed and hungry for revenge. It was as though Ruru, like himself, had been delivered from a curse. He had learned at last to love all things. His anger had left him; in its place was a warm and gentle compassion towards all living creatures, and they in turn learned to draw near him and answer his call. Dundubha thanked heaven for the miracle.

161

But though his anger had gone, there still remained, in Ruru's heart, an aching grief for the girl he had lost. Though many days had passed he could not forget his Pramadvara. Indeed, it seemed to Ruru that time, instead of healing his sorrow, had only sharpened it.

'You must go home to your parents now,' Dundubha told Ruru one day. 'It is many days since you left them, and they are longing for your return.'

Ruru agreed, and the two friends started out. As they walked they spoke of all the things they had experienced together. They were very near Ruru's village when Dundubha commented: 'All creatures have the right to live out their days in peace.' And Ruru hearing him remembered his Pramadvara with a stab of pain.

'All creatures . . . yes,' he exclaimed sorrowfully. 'And yet . . . Dundubha, Pramadvara's life was taken from her in its sweetest hour.'

Dundubha glanced at him. The lines of bitterness had gone from Ruru's face; the hardness had vanished from his mouth and eyes. Dundubha was well satisfied with what he saw. Now he began to speak to him again and, this time, Dundubha spoke of the great mystery that is life and the greater one that is death. He spoke of the destinies of living creatures that the gods determine for them at the time of their birth. He explained to Ruru the philosophies of life and death that saints and holy men had propounded through the ages. Ruru listened attentively but continued to mourn his beloved.

'So young,' he repeated brokenly, 'so young and innocent! Oh, what would I not give to see her again!'

Dundubha stopped and turned suddenly to face him: 'And what will you give, Ruru, to have your Pramadvara restored to you?' he asked. There was a smile on his lips but his gaze was intense.

Ruru sighed: 'Dundubha, my friend, you have done much for me, and now you must go your way and I must go mine. I have learned much from you . . . but to talk of Pramadvara's return is meaningless. We must not indulge in idle dreams.'

But Dundubha repeated gravely: 'What will you give, Ruru, what will you give?' Ruru cried out, covering his face with his hands: 'Oh, what would I not give . . . .' Tears flowed down his cheeks, for his grief was as fresh as it had been on the day that Pramadvara had died. Then he ran from Dundubha saying: 'Go away, holy man; don't mock my grief. No one can help me now.'

But Dundubha would not go. He followed Ruru and he gripped his shoulder, 'Would you be willing to give up half your life for that of your bride, Ruru? Tell me, would you?'

'Willingly, willingly,' Ruru said, 'Let the gods take half my years. Without Pramadvara what will they bring me but sorrow?' He looked up at Dundubha with a sudden, wild hope.

'It is all a matter of destiny,' he heard Dundubha murmur. 'Long ago when the gods were creating Pramadvara, Yama laid claim to her, declaring that he would carry her off to his kingdom in her youth. But the gods persuaded him to make a bargain with them. He agreed to release her on one condition—that someone give up half his years for her life.'

'Let her have the years of my life,' Ruru cried and he prayed as he had never prayed before. So lost in prayer was he that he did not feel Dundubha lay his hand upon his head in blessing, 'Let it be so.' Nor did he know when his kind friend went away and vanished into the depths of the forest.

He was still on his knees with his eyes closed, when there came to his ears the joyful voices of people calling his name. 'Ruru, come home! Pramadvara has returned from the dead and we are preparing for your wedding.' In a daze he saw them as they crowded round him. Still in a daze he felt himself lifted upon their shoulders as they sang and cheered and carried him home to his loved one, his bride, the beautiful Pramadvara.

9

Markandeya and Yama

There was once an old couple who longed to have children. They had spent all their days in prayer hoping to have their wish fulfilled. Many years passed until one day the gods relented and appeared before them. 'We have come to bless you,' said the gods, 'and grant you your desire.'

They held out their gracious hands in blessing—hands which the old couple knew could pour out the bounty men strive for—wealth and good fortune, empire, power, success. The man and his wife were so overwhelmed by the vision that they could scarcely speak, but the gods smiled kindly and begged them to name their desire. At last the mortals found their voice and cried out to the gods to give them children. 'Children,' they pleaded with the heavenly ones. 'Children to cheer our lonely lives and light our way to heaven.'

The gods smiled indulgently. They seemed at first willing to grant their prayer, then to hesitate and grow doubtful.

'The gods grant gifts,' they murmured softly. 'But always with a condition attached. They grant men's desires, yes—but they also put the men they favour to a test. And we must put you to a test now, before we grant you your wish.' They paused and then continued:

'We could give you many children, or we could give you an only child. You must choose.'

To the man and his wife it seemed, when they heard this, that all heaven had opened about them. They loved children so greatly that if they had been given a hundred they would gladly have had them all.

But the gods had not finished speaking:

'We could give you a hundred sons,' they said, as if they had read the mortals' thoughts, 'each of whom would live a hundred years, but they would be bad, wicked men. Or we could give you one son alone who would be full of goodness.'

'That is easy,' thought the human creatures. It seemed to them obvious as daylight that they would take the good child! How could it be otherwise? But the gods had not done with them.

'Wait,' they warned, holding up their hands and smiling remotely, mysteriously, 'there is something else. The life span of this good child will be a bare sixteen years, while your hundred wicked sons, remember, will each live a hundred years and more! And now,' they concluded triumphantly, 'you may choose: will you have many wicked sons who will be long-lived and prosperous, or one good child who will live only for sixteen short years?'

The old man and his wife looked at each other and then at the heavenly beings, aghast. Surely the gods could not be so cruel! But the shining ones continued to smile as they stood before the helpless mortals. Their eyes, remote and calm, did not blink or move.

'Choose, now, good mortals,' was all they whispered, smiling. Their voices were as soft as the movement of stars in the heavens. In the end the old couple made their bitter choice.

'Give us the one boy who will live a good life,' they said and went on sorrowfully, ' and if he is to live only till he is sixteen, then let it be so, for that is the will of heaven!'

The gods were pleased. 'You have chosen well.' They blessed the couple and vanished into the air. Shortly afterwards, a boy was born to the couple. They named him Markandeya.

As he grew, the parents saw how the words of the gods were coming true: there was a happiness and a radiance in the child that drew all people, all creatures, to him. The very earth and sky seemed to smile in welcome at his birth; his mother's heart swelled with joy as she pressed the baby to her, while pride glowed in his father's gentle face. The neighbours came in to see the golden boy and showered him with love. Markandeya grew sturdy and handsome and learnt to play with the village children. In the evenings when the lamps were lit and the cows safe in their sheds, his mother sang to him and told him tales of gods and heroes, ghosts and witches, of talking animals and magic, and mystery and wonder. In the cool of each morning his father took him by the hand and led him to the fields to watch the oxen plough the earth and turn the soil. Together they saw the planting; they watched the seasons change; and when the fields turned golden with ripe grain the boy helped the villagers gather the harvest.

Markandeya brought to his parents a happiness they had never known before. And yet, all the while, deep in their hearts, a secret sorrow gnawed at them. How could they forget that fateful meeting with the gods?

164

Markandeya sensed their grief, and wondered about its cause. What was this burden his parents carried? Why did his mother turn her face suddenly from his to wipe away that secret tear? What was the darkness that clouded his father's eyes? Sometimes in the stillness of the night, Markandeya woke to hear the sound of his parents' muffled weeping. He sensed that it had to do with him. He began to listen more carefully, to piece together the small scraps of conversation he sometimes overheard. He saw how they hung charms and talismans round his neck, how they brought him sacred ash in lockets, whispering that it had magical powers over life and death; how they consulted palmists and astrologers and bearded men in saffron clothes who called themselves wise and holy. And then, one day, in a flash, Markandeya realized what it was all about. He spoke to his parents about it and they confessed. Yes, it was death they feared . . . his death.

Death! he had seen death . . . the death of leaf and flower in the fullness of their growth. He had seen the death of birds and butterflies; he and his friends had stopped their play to watch processions of men softly chanting the name of god, as they carried the stiff, cold body of a friend on a bier to the burning-ground. Sometimes the body was shrouded in white; sometimes in gaudy red and yellow, with marigold and jasmine garlands laid on it. Sometimes there was music and dancing; always there was weeping.

He remembered what people said about death: death was cruel; death was kind; death was release; death was frightening; death was the finality, the end of all things. Death seemed to be a great puzzle. For what happened after death no man could tell. Death brought grief and tears and a searing anguish to the hearts of those whom the dead left behind. Death was feared. Its very name was avoided. His parents were afraid. They who had seemed to him so grown up and strong and wise were helpless and afraid in the face of death!

They had no answer and so he must find the answer for them. They were frightened; so he must give them confidence and hope. He must not die. He must live for them.

Markandeya began to wander away from his youthful companions. His mind was full of questions. He needed silence in which he could wrestle with himself to find the answers. The realization came to him, one day, that if he discovered Shiva, the god of eternity, whose dance, they said, brought about the end of all things, then he might find out from him the answer to death.

So he sat before the symbol of Shiva in worship, eyes closed, all his boyish games and pranks forgotten. Through the day and through the night the boy Markandeya sat unmoving as if he was carved of stone. As the weeks passed, and he went deeper into silence the need for food and nourishment and all things left him. The seasons changed around him, the months rolled by. The grass and weeds grew tall about him where he sat. Insects buzzed around his head. Snakes slid up and down his form, but he felt nothing, for his mind and all his being were fixed on Shiva.

The gods looked down from heaven where the power of his meditation reached them.

'Markandeya at prayer?' they whispered to each other, sorely troubled. 'Men must not think so deeply or pray so hard. If men's minds turn to contemplation of the eternal, then what will become of us? We are the givers of good things, wealth, earthly happiness, power. People pray to us because they desire these things. Where would our power be if men came to realize that our gifts are unreal? What would happen to us if mortals came to understand that only the eternal is true?'

But then they remembered that Markandeya had not long to live, and the thought comforted them. Soon Markandeya would be sixteen, and at sixteen he would die!

His parents remembered it too in their lonely cottage, and wept. In his kingdom of the dead, Yama stopped brooding as he too remembered that the time had nearly come to claim the boy; while deep inside him, Markandeya knew without words that a great change was about to take place in his life.

On the day that he was sixteen the messengers of Yama came to Markandeya. They stood a little way off, and called him.

'Come Markandeya,' they said softly, enticingly. 'Come, for your time is up.' Deep in prayer, Markandeya did not hear them. They called louder: 'Come, come!' But there was no answer from him, no movement. They stared at him in surprise—the messengers of death were used to being obeyed instantly! Then they saw the peace and strength in Markandeya's face and they trembled, turned pale and dared not approach him. Instead they turned and fled back to their master in a panic.

'He sits before the Shiva symbol,' they cried to Yama, 'and we dare not touch him.' Yama looked at their white face and chattering teeth and could not understand it at all.

'My power defied? My command flouted?' He arose and drew himself up to his great height, while the ghosts and shadows that

peopled his kingdom flapped their wings and shrieked and cursed. 'Fools!' he thundered at his servants. 'Where is your pride, your dignity? Have you surrendered to a mere boy?'

But they shrank away, cowering, and begged to be spared. Yama glared at them, cursed them for cowards and fools, but in the end he knew that he must go himself to fetch Markandeya. They were losing time, and no creature may outlive the hour of his death. That was the law of the universe.

Yama looked into the great book in which the names of his victims were inscribed. His finger, flashing with jewelled rings, followed one line. '*Markandeya*,' he read, '*must die when he reaches his sixteenth year.*' The gods had decreed. Yama untethered the dark, horned buffalo on which he rode; from the hook on the wall he lifted the rope with which he made the noose for dead men's souls; and he set out from his kingdom, while the death drums boomed and flocks of vultures rose up crying in shrill, weird voices.

Then Yama, riding his buffalo, and holding the fatal noose in his hand, approached the spot where Markandeya sat, and halted. He alighted from the buffalo. He tied it to a tree and, with the rope in his hand, he advanced. A few paces away he paused deliberately. Fixing his red-rimmed eye on Markandeya he called:

'Young mortal, your time has come. You must put all things by and follow me.' And at that exact instant Markandeya was sixteen. Without opening his eyes he smiled gravely.

'I am at prayer, Yama,' he answered. 'You must wait a little for me, until I have finished.'

Yama laughed: 'Wait?' The great beetling eyebrows rose. 'Wait, did you say? Do you not know that Yama waits for no one? Do you not know me?'

'Indeed I do,' Markandeya answered smiling. 'You are death. You are very great and very powerful. I know that. But you are not greater than Shiva the eternal. Wait for a while and I shall come when I have finished my worship.'

'Ha,' said Yama, advancing menacingly. 'You puny creature of flesh and blood; you who own nothing, and stand alone in your weakness, do you dare to defy me, before whom kings, emperors, and mighty warriors tremble and shiver? Has Yama ever gone back defeated and empty-handed?' With a terrible laugh the god of death flung the noose around Markandeya's neck. And he stood there with the end of the rope in his hand and said, his voice growing kinder now: 'All is over, Markandeya. You are mine now, and you will have to follow me into my kingdom.'

At that moment a great surge of weeping, cries of mourning, groans of protest and sorrow rose up around him. Yama shook his head, for he knew those cries well; wherever he went they followed him, as the helpless folk begged him yet again not to take away some loved one.

'What has been decreed,' said Yama, in a lordly voice, 'cannot be altered. Come, mortal, come . . . .'

Yama stood waiting, one impatient foot tapping the dusty earth. He continued to hear the cries. All things were the same to him and all creatures were alike. Nevertheless he gave ear. This time the cries—surely they were different? He frowned. What was the strange unease within him? From every side he could hear weeping, and to the voices of humanfolk were added, this time, the cries of all living creatures. The very grasses wept.

'Do not take Markandeya, Yama! Do not take him!' That was what they all said. Yama turned, with a slight shrug of his shoulders, 'Fate,' he reasoned, sighing, 'the will of the gods . . . no man may outlive his time . . . no man.' And he pulled gently at the rope, then paused. He pictured Markandeya walking alongside him with the noose around his neck—a gentle boy, brave, beautiful, wise. His radiance would light their path . . . . Already he loved him, wanted to possess him. 'Markandeya,' he whispered the name softly. But nothing happened. With a slight start Yama realized that Markandeya had not risen, was not walking towards him. 'It is not possible,' Yama murmured, eyebrows lifting with surprise. 'It cannot be.'

Yet he knew it was. The noose was around Markandeya's neck and though he, Yama, had pulled it, nothing had happened. Markandeya sat deep in meditation beside the symbol of Shiva. Yama's command had not reached him at all. Puzzled, Yama looked down at the rope he held in his hand. In his mind's eye he saw the vast numbers of people it had dragged since the beginning of time and taken into the region of the dead. What had gone wrong now? Why did the victim not move? Yama felt a tiny flutter of fear.

He tugged again, a second time. Never before had he needed to do that. But nothing happened, nothing, even this second time. His brow knit with worry. He pulled again and again. His attendants eyed him fearfully; he could feel their ghoulish glances scan his face, question his power and strength. He bit his lip, braced himself, and drawing a deep breath, he pulled once more. Then yet again. Nothing, nothing moved. Time stood still while Markandeya sat in meditation.

'Strange,' muttered Yama, puzzled and confused, but unwilling to show it. He turned round furtively. This too, was something he had never done. He had never before needed to look a second time. And now when he looked he saw a sight that startled and scared him. Markandeya sat there with his hands upon the Shiva symbol, and his eyes closed. . . and the whole earth was around him—all living creatures—praying to Shiva to save Markandeya from Yama's clutches.

'I will frighten them,' thought Yama, and opened the eyes of the mortals so that they saw his terrible form and recognized him. At once the mortals fell on their faces and implored him to spare Markandeya.

Yama began to laugh. 'How can that be?' he answered them. 'His time has come and no man may outlive his time. Remember the law of nature, foolish ones, and go back to your homes; Markandeya belongs to me.'

'We are not concerned with the law of nature,' cried the people sadly. 'Markandeya belongs to us, for we love him. He is good and pure, innocent and young. He is too young to die! Yama, spare him!'

Yama replied laughing: 'It is the decree of the gods, the will of heaven. No creature may outlive its time. Do you not understand that that is the law of the universe?'

'Markandeya is too young, too good to die,' sobbed the people.

'All things live by the law,' Yama argued. 'The heavenly bodies revolve in accordance with the law. The very gods are subject to the law. Even I, death, am not excepted, for death itself must one day die. The law is supreme!'

'But Markandeya . . . .' began the weeping people. They turned their eyes and hearts to heaven again and prayed. Such was the strength and power of their prayer that Yama saw the heavens open and Shiva descend from the snow-bound heights of Kailasa to where Markandeya sat with the noose of death about his neck.

There were cries of wonder. 'Do something, lord. Do something,' pleaded the people. 'Save Markandeya!'

'Against death?' Shiva asked doubtfully. 'Would that be wise?'

'Wise?' echoed the people. 'Shiva, we love Markandeya. He is good. What will become of us if he goes from us?'

But Shiva looked troubled. 'Death is a part of life,' he said to them. 'How can you separate the two?' But the people clamoured all around him, crying out to him to spare Markandeya.

'What do you want me to do?' said Shiva at last. All the people looked around them, thinking hard. Then at last, a few clever ones came up with an idea: 'Lord,' they said, 'you could annihilate death! You could remove death from earth. For Markandeya's sake you could do this.'

Enthusiastically, everyone took up the idea with one voice. The whole earth resounded with their cries. 'Yes, yes, Shiva. Annihilate death! Remove it entirely. That will solve the problem.' The people were very pleased with themselves. What a marvellous idea! What a clever thing to think of! The annihilation of death—the end of tears and sorrows. What a perfect plan to present!

They saw Yama sneer, and yet alarm shadowed his eyes. They saw Shiva shake his head. His face still showed doubt. They saw him turn to Yama.

'Overlook the law, Yama,' they heard him plead. 'For Markandeya make an exception.'

But Yama regained his composure and looked insolently into Shiva's face. 'There can be no exception,' Yama snapped. 'Fate has decreed, and no one can change fate.'

'No one!' repeated Shiva, and in the sudden breathless silence even the leaves stopped their rustle. 'Are you not aware Yama, of mortals who have grappled with fate and changed its course?'

'Markandeya is mine,' Yama said loudly, changing the subject. 'He will follow me into the region of the dead.'

'You may not take him.' Shiva's voice was quiet; very quiet. His eyes shone like twin suns, while the mortals held their breath.

'Who is there that can stop me?' Defiant and haughty, Yama began to draw in the length of his rope. He came very close to Markandeya.

'Will you disobey me, godling?' Shiva spoke quietly, almost in a whisper.

Yama twirled the ends of his moustache. Pride glowed in his fierce eyes. 'I am the god of death,' he thundered, 'and I am no one's slave. Stand back, Shiva, for Markandeya belongs to me. Even you shall not come between us!'

'Shall not?' Shiva echoed ominously. 'Shall not, did you say, Yama? Have you grown so proud and insolent, then, you little god? Has your power gone to your crowned head?'

'What can you do?' swaggered Yama. 'Death is all-powerful.' He looked terrible as he said it. His form seemed to fill the universe. 'Death is everywhere. What can you do, Shiva, even though you are the god of eternity?'

'Be careful, Yama,' Shiva warned. 'For Markandeya's sake I can do what the people say—annihilate death. Once and for all I can bring your power and your empire to an end, your pride to dust.'

Yama began to laugh. 'My power will never end!' he said scornfully. The people stared breathlessly. What would happen now? The two mighty ones faced each other. Their giant forms filled the earth and sky. Between them sat Markandeya, his eyes closed in deep meditation. And the small and frightened people were quite forgotten in this conflict. As they looked, they saw Shiva move

forward, lift his leg and kick Yama in the chest, so that the god of death staggered and fell sprawling on the earth. His crown slipped and fell in the dust. Shiva stood over him.

'Your power has been stripped from you, Yama,' his voice rang out and echoed from all sides. 'Go from here and hide your face. Henceforth there shall be no death!' Slowly and painfully, Yama staggered to his feet, and he was now just a shrunken, frightened little shadow.

'So be it,' he murmured. His voice rose scarcely above a whisper: 'So be it, Shiva. Henceforth there shall be no death.' Then, with bent head and leading his buffalo, he retraced his steps to his kingdom of darkness.

172

'No death, no death!' shouted the people triumphantly. 'Our prayer has been answered. We have won. Henceforth no one shall die, for Markandeya has conquered death.'

'Death has been conquered, yes,' said Shiva. 'But perhaps the solution is not so simple.' But no one heard him—everyone was dancing and singing with joy. Shiva went back to Kailasa, and no one noticed him go in the general rejoicing. And all the while, Markandeya sat in meditation and knew nothing of what had happened.

Yama stayed in his country and his days were idle. Death would

no longer claim lives. Now, all creatures, all people, would live for ever. No more death—only birth. No ending—only a beginning, and a continuing on and on and on.

And so it happened. Now there was only life—spawning, squirming, pulsating, teeming life; life from every particle of vapour, every speck of water, pushing out from every crack, every crevice, every pore of the rich and fecund earth. Day followed night and night followed day, as weeks and months went by. The people who had cried out for death's defeat looked about them and saw everywhere things being born, things growing—plants, leaves, insects, reptiles, birds, animals, human beings—never ceasing, never dying. New leaves sprouted on the trees, but the old, the withered, the decayed remained on the boughs, growing older, decaying further, but not falling off in the fullness of their time. Flowers bloomed and fruit ripened and rotted and rotted. But they lived on. Insects multiplied, and the swarms hid the light of the sun. So too the birds and animals. So too human creatures. Their numbers increased, a hundred and thousandfold, for the old and the sick, the diseased and the feeble lived on with the healthy, the happy, the young and the strong. The tired ones longed for rest. Those in pain cried out to be released. But there was no end to pain, no end to suffering, for there was no end to life. There was only creation, birth and growth.

'This is no blessing!' cried the people in terror. 'It was better when death walked among us; far, far better.' And they cried out to death and begged him to end their agony.

'What can I do?' Yama asked them sullenly. 'It was you who wanted it so. I could not disobey Shiva's command.'

To Shiva then the people went, begging him to take back this blessing—this was no blessing at all, but a curse. Shiva turned to them. His face was very stern—but there was a kindly twinkle in the depths of his eyes.

'It is good that you have learnt a lesson,' Shiva said, 'and good, too, that Yama has learnt his—that he is not all-powerful; that Shiva who is the eternal one, can conquer even death.'

His voice grew gentler as he continued, 'But go now and pray to Yama. Take him my command and beg him to return again among mortals.'

Greatly chastened, the people went to Yama with Shiva's mandate, and a sadder but wiser Yama smiled compassionately at them. 'I will come back,' he promised them. Then he paused, hesitating. 'But there is still the question of Markandeya,' he reminded them at last. 'I have not solved his problem yet.'

'Yes,' answered the people remembering. 'There is still the question of Markandeya. That is how it all started.'

But when they went with Yama to the place where Markandeya had sat in prayer, they discovered that there was no Markandeya there; only the song of birds, the hum of bees and dragonflies, the murmur of flowing water; only the sunshine filtering through the rustling leaves; only the breezes blowing. Beyond that, there was no sound, but the silence of the eternal into which he had merged.

174

Special Notes on the Colour Plates

No. 1 (facing page 2): *Astika and the Snake Maidens*
The nether world of nagas or the snake people is traditionally considered the repository of precious gems and hidden treasures. It is the radiance of these minerals which illuminate the subterranean darkness.

No. 2 (facing page 20): *The Nagas*
The Nagas with their half human bodies symbolize the human acceptance of reptilian grace and wisdom. The snake in Hindu myth also stands for fertility and renewal.

No. 3 (facing page 30): *King Ashwapati and the Astrologers*
Marriage in India is traditionally based on compatible horoscopes. As the astrologer, usually a learned brahmin, sits down to chart the horoscope, he is welcomed with fruit, coconuts and the auspicious betel leaf.

No. 4 (facing page 38): *Yama and Savitri*
The solemnity and awesomeness of the journey to the land of the dead is heightened in this picture by Yama's austere appearance, his grey and stern visage and his ominous stare.

No. 5 (facing page 56): *Hiranyaksha and Varaha*
Vishnu, the Preserver, in the Hindu pantheon, took various incarnations to restore the balance between good and evil. Varaha, the Boar, is one such incarnation—immense and deadly.

No. 6 (facing page 72): *Narasimha and Hiranyakashipu*
The Man–Lion, Narasimha is Vishnu's fiercest incarnation. The angry reds in this picture are tempered by the saffron and gold of divine deliverance. The protruding red tongue of the wrathful god presages the destruction of evil in the person of Hiranyakashipu.

No. 7 (facing page 82): *Shiva and Sati*
Pictured in this colour plate is the simple and idyllic domesticity of Sati's life with Shiva, with the faithful bull, Nandi, Shiva's mount as their companion.

No. 8 (facing page 102): *Uma, the Young Devotee*
Uma, on her way to the temple of Shiva, carries the traditional offerings of water, fruit and incense.

No. 9 (facing page 108): *The Messengers of Love*
The austere Himalayan landscape of Shiva's abode blossoms into spring with the presence of Vasanta. Kama, the god of love, aims his flower-tipped arrow at Shiva. Note the emblem above Kama's pennant: the fish—a symbol of fertility and attraction. Also note the parrot, Kama's mount, perched in the flowering Ashoka tree.

No. 10 (facing page 120): *Chand Saudagar and Manasa*
The peace and serenity of the merchant's garden is disturbed by the brooding presence of Manasa Devi.

No. 11 (facing page 130): *The Bridal Chamber*
The sombre hues of this picture reflect the nocturnal mood. Note the canopied and flower-strewn bed and soft lamplight—symbols of the nuptial night.

No. 12 (facing page 142): *Shukra, Kacha and Devayani*
Shukra, the teacher of the asuras, is known in Indian mythology as the guiding spirit of learning and the fine arts. He is here shown receiving Kacha who comes in search of knowledge—as is denoted in the picture by the palm-leaf manuscripts in their hands. Shukra's weakness for wine is shown by the little wine-pot and ladle.

No. 13 (facing page 158): *Ruru and Dundubha*
The dramatic scene in which Dundubha turns from snake to sage is pictured in the contrast between the dark earth and the living green.

No. 14 (facing page 166): *A Hymn to Shiva*
This colour plate shows Markandeya totally immersed in worship of Shiva. The enshrined lingam, in the picture, is the symbol of the god.

The composition of this picture, with the overarching tree, reinforces the closed and private world of the boy's utter devotion.